MORE PRAISE FOR *THE QUALITY CURE*

"Cutler's insights are illuminating ... a must-read for those who care about real improvement in our health care system."

—Richard M. Scheffler, Distinguished Professor of Health Economics and Public Policy at the University of California, Berkeley

"In *Your Money or Your Life*, David Cutler taught the world that the rapid rise in health care spending over the past forty years has been worth it. In *The Quality Cure,* he takes the next step, showing us how we can control the burden of health care costs while increasing quality. This book is a treasure trove of critical facts about what works and what doesn't in health care, and of invaluable insights about how to translate those facts into practice. In a policy arena fraught with zero-sum solutions, Cutler reminds us that we can have our quality and afford it too."

—Jonathan Gruber, Professor of Economics, Massachusetts Institute of Technology

The Quality Cure

THE AARON WILDAVSKY FORUM FOR PUBLIC POLICY

Edited by Lee Friedman

This series is intended to sustain the intellectual excitement that Aaron Wildavsky created for scholars of public policy everywhere. The ideas in each volume are initially presented and discussed at a public lecture and forum held at the University of California.

AARON WILDAVSKY, 1930–1993

"Your prolific pen has brought real politics to the study of budgeting, to the analysis of myriad public policies, and to the discovery of the values underlying the political cultures by which peoples live. You have improved every institution with which you have been associated, notably Berkeley's Graduate School of Public Policy, which as Founding Dean you quickened with your restless innovative energy. Advocate of freedom, mentor to policy analysts everywhere." (Yale University, May 1993, from text granting the honorary degree of Doctor of Social Science)

1. *Missing Persons: A Critique of Personhood in the Social Sciences,* by Mary Douglas and Steven Ney
2. *The Bridge over the Racial Divide: Rising Inequality and Coalition Politics,* by William Julius Wilson
3. *The New Public Management: Improving Research and Policy Dialogue,* by Michael Barzelay
4. *Falling Behind: How Rising Inequality Harms the Middle Class,* by Robert H. Frank
5. *Godly Republic: A Centrist Civic Blueprint for America's Faith-Based Future,* by John J. DiIulio, Jr.
6. *Bounded Rationality and Politics,* by Jonathan Bendor
7. *Taxing the Poor: Doing Damage to the Truly Disadvantaged,* by Katherine S. Newman and Rourke L. O'Brien
8. *Changing Inequality,* by Rebecca M. Blank
9. *The Quality Cure: How Focusing on Health Care Quality Can Save Your Life and Lower Spending Too,* by David Cutler

The Quality Cure

How Focusing on Health Care Quality Can Save Your Life and Lower Spending Too

David Cutler

UNIVERSITY OF CALIFORNIA PRESS
Berkeley Los Angeles London

University of California Press, one of the most distinguished university presses in the United States, enriches lives around the world by advancing scholarship in the humanities, social sciences, and natural sciences. Its activities are supported by the UC Press Foundation and by philanthropic contributions from individuals and institutions. For more information, visit www.ucpress.edu.

University of California Press
Berkeley and Los Angeles, California

University of California Press, Ltd.
London, England

Library of Congress Cataloging-in-Publication Data

Cutler, David.
The quality cure : how focusing on health care quality can save your life and lower spending too / David Cutler.
pages cm — (Wildavsky Forum series ; 9)
Includes bibliographical references and index.
ISBN 978-0-520-28199-8 (cloth : alk. paper)
ISBN 978-0-520-28200-1 (pbk. : alk. paper)
ISBN 978-0-520-95776-3 (e-book)
1. Medical care. 2. Medical care—Quality control. 3. Outcome assessment (Medical care) I. Title.
RA399.A1C87 2014
362.1—dc23
2013040183

Manufactured in the United States of America

23 22 21 20 19 18 17 16
10 9 8 7 6 5 4 3 2

In keeping with a commitment to support environmentally responsible and sustainable printing practices, UC Press has printed this book on Natures Natural, a fiber that contains 30% post-consumer waste and meets the minimum requirements of ANSI/NISO Z39.48-1992 (R 1997) (*Permanence of Paper*).

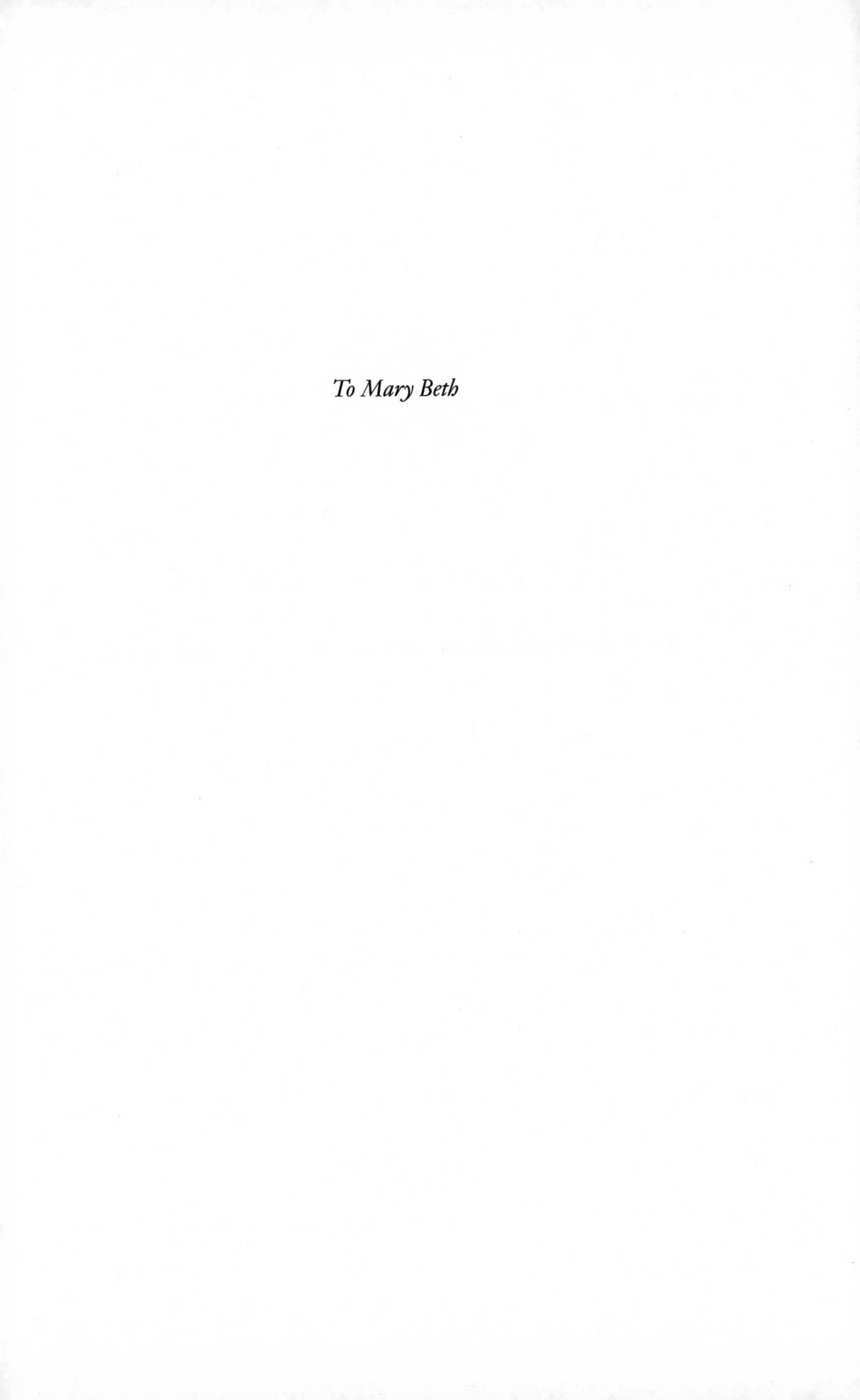

To Mary Beth

CONTENTS

ILLUSTRATIONS

FIGURES

TABLES

ACKNOWLEDGMENTS

The thoughts and words in this book are mine, but many people helped along the way. Lee Friedman invited me to give the Aaron Wildavsky lecture at the University of California, Berkeley, which was the impetus for this volume. I remain grateful for his invitation. Many colleagues influenced my thinking over the years. They are too numerous to name, but I thank them all. Shaira Bhanji provided fantastic research and editing help. The title of this book is taken from a *New York Times Magazine* article by Roger Lowenstein, which touched on my views about health care. I am grateful to Roger for the article and for allowing me to use the title. The National Institute on Aging supported virtually all my research on the topics in this book; I am extremely grateful to them. Finally, I thank you, the reader, for being interested in one of the most difficult and fascinating challenges of our time.

PREFACE

For decades, health care was like the weather—everybody talked about it, but nobody did anything about it. Talk was easy; politicians and analysts of all stripes agreed that we wanted a health care system focused on preventing disease whenever possible and treating it appropriately when necessary. Hand-holding sessions between people of different backgrounds pledging to work together for these goals were easy to arrange.

In the past half decade, talk has turned into action. In 2006, Massachusetts became the first state to guarantee near-universal coverage, and the federal government followed suit four years later. The Patient Protection and Affordable Care Act of 2010 was the farthest-reaching piece of social legislation in half a century.

Alas, action is more controversial than talk. Conservatives universally opposed the Affordable Care Act—not a single Republican voted for it—and liberals nearly universally supported it. The public is just as divided as Congress. About 40 percent of the population likes the Affordable Care Act, virtually the same share opposes it, and the rest are undecided. The division between those on the left and right runs so deep that we can't even agree on what to call the bill. Is it the Patient Protection and Affordable Care Act or Obamacare?

What can possibly be said about health care after the Affordable Care Act controversy? A lot, it turns out. I want to return to the question that motivated the consensus in the first place: can we have a better-functioning health care system, and if so, what would it look like? I have been researching this question for some time, and I believe a better system is within our reach. I describe what it would look like in this volume.

The book has two broad parts. In the first three chapters, I discuss the central public policy concerns about medical care, focusing on costs. Among the key lessons in this part of the book is the importance of creating value. Our goal should be not merely to lower our spending on medical care, but to do so by increasing the value that our dollars bring. Many existing proposals are not likely to accomplish this.

In the remaining five chapters, I present the quality cure. There are many interventions in health care that will raise the quality of care and simultaneously lower its cost, but it will require transforming the system to realize these gains. I discuss the central building blocks of value improvement in health care: use of information technology, realigned payment systems, and value-focused organizations.

The book covers a lot of intellectual territory. As might be imagined, there is a voluminous literature on many of the topics I cover. I review the best of that literature, as I see it. I do not address studies that I believe to be poorly designed or badly executed. Thus, this book is not a comprehensive index of every topic covered. Further, as befits a scholar, I draw my own conclusions from the data. Clearly, not all readers will agree with everything I write. I try to indicate where other views differ from mine, but I may not detail every instance. I ask forgiveness in advance.

• • •

This is not a book about politics, but politics necessarily intrudes on occasion. How can it not? On such a heated topic, it is incumbent upon an author to be forthright about his views. Here are mine. I was President Obama's senior health care advisor in his 2008 presidential campaign. I advised him on many of the issues that became part of the Affordable Care Act, and I was an informal campaign advisor in 2012. Before that, I worked on President Clinton's health plan and advised the presidential campaign of Bill Bradley. End of confession.

That said, this is not a book urging support for or opposition to the Affordable Care Act. Americans have likely heard all they want to about that topic. Rather, it is a look at the challenges that policy faces in health care and how we can surmount them.

Politics did have an interesting role in the preparation of this manuscript. I started working on this volume in 2011, before the Supreme Court ruled on the constitutionality of the Affordable Care Act and a year ahead of an election that focused heavily on whether Obamacare should be repealed. At the time, I didn't know whether the book should take the Affordable Care Act as a given or talk about its replacement. As the research and writing continued, the Supreme Court upheld the law, and the American population voted Barack Obama back into the presidency. I believe that is good for the country—and it had the side benefit of making my analysis to that point still relevant.

Along the way, other changes occurred, as they always do. Major legislative efforts to control costs were enacted in

Arkansas, Massachusetts, and Oregon, and other states are considering similar changes. I had some role in drafting the legislation in Massachusetts and now in its implementation, so that helped me refine my thinking. The early effects of the Affordable Care Act are being felt, and that too factored into my views. Clearly, this book is topical. Fortunately, there is more to health care than the day-to-day machinations of government policy.

There is an old Chinese proverb, "May you live in interesting times." On the legislative front, I very much hope the times will become less interesting. The past few years have seen the most substantive changes in health care legislation in a generation. Our job now is to digest these changes and make the new system work. One way to assess this book is as a road map showing how the new system should operate. Just as I do for all maps, I hope it is accurate.

David Cutler
Cambridge, May 2013

CHAPTER ONE

Cost, Access, and Quality

The Three Horsemen of the Apocalypse

"What do you think are the top two problems with the nation's medical care system?" In a June 2009 survey, approximately one thousand Americans were asked this question. Over half the respondents cited cost as one of their top two concerns. This mirrors results from April 2007 and March 2008, when the same question was asked to a different group of people, but the same answers were given.[1] Costs appeared in various guises—from concern about prescription drug prices and the high costs of hospital and physician care to overall insurance costs. One way or another, the price tag of medical care is what worries people most.

Access comes in second. One-third of Americans worry about people who do not have insurance coverage or people whose coverage is not sufficiently generous. The third concern is the quality of care. One in ten people cite poor service, lack of quality health care, or other quality problems in their top two agenda items.

Cost, access, and quality are not just what Americans fear about health care, but also what experts highlight as the core issues in our health care system. Analysts from both the Left and the Right decry the high cost, limited access, and haphazard quality of American medicine. According to an article written by Stuart Butler of the right-of-center Heritage Foundation and Henry Aaron of the left-of-center Brookings Institution, "For at least 20 years, commentators have bewailed the lack of adequate health insurance among growing numbers of Americans. For an even longer time, analysts and experts have warned that health care costs were rising unsustainably. Yet no consensus has formed on what to do about these twin adversities.... Meanwhile, the ranks of the uninsured swell, health costs soar, and states and businesses cut benefits."[2] Indeed, these two analysts even wrote a paper together, arguing for liberal state experimentation to address these problems.

Politicians heard the message. The much-maligned health reform bill of President Obama's first term, colloquially known as Obamacare but officially named the Patient Protection and Affordable Care Act—or simply the Affordable Care Act, as I shall call it—was designed by President Barack Obama to address these issues. As President Obama said when introducing his health care legislation, "The plan I'm announcing tonight would meet three basic goals. It will provide more security and stability to those who have health insurance. It will provide insurance for those who don't. And it will slow the growth of health care costs for our families, our businesses, and our government."[3] And though Republicans criticized the legislation, they did not attack those goals. According to Mitch McConnell, the Senate minority leader, "Look, nobody is satisfied with the health care system as it is. We've got serious problems that need to be addressed. Costs are out of control. Too many people are being squeezed out of the market.... We can do better. We can expand access to people with preexisting conditions. We can keep people from being kicked off their plans. We can lower costs and premiums. We can do all of these things without undermining the things we do best and without raising taxes that kill jobs in a bad economy."[4] Politicians know what people want, even when they can't convince people they have the answers.

• • •

Cost, access, and quality all need to be addressed. But these problems are not equally difficult to solve. Start with access. Fifty million Americans have gone without insurance coverage for the entirety of a year,[5] and about as many are uninsured at some point during a year.[6] That means that every year, one in three Americans experience some sort of an uninsured spell.

Uninsured people are without coverage largely because of affordability and accessibility issues. The dominant response of the uninsured, when asked why they don't have coverage, is that they cannot afford it.[7] In addition, many uninsured do not even know how or where to buy coverage. The affordability concern is particularly salient because health insurance is so expensive. The average cost of a family health insurance policy is about $15,700, and a single policy is about $5,600.[8] That is an enormous hurdle for all but the highest-income families.

On top of the large number of uninsured, even those with insurance feel insecure: they worry that their insurance will not cover the services they need, their premiums will increase if they or a family member gets sick, or they will be dropped from coverage entirely if their income falls (perhaps because they lose their job) or their medical bills rise.

These access issues have real consequences. Twenty percent of people indicate that there was a time during the past year when they or a family member needed medical care but did not receive it; the most common reason is financial.[9] And the Institute of Medicine estimates that 18,000 deaths per year could be avoided if everyone had insurance.[10]

Given the grave results of lack of access to care, it is ironic that covering the uninsured is not nearly as difficult as many believe. Some type of subsidy or tax credit is needed to make health insurance affordable for those with moderate incomes. In addition, a (virtual) location needs to be established where people can shop for plans. In fact, designing a tax credit for health insurance is relatively straightforward: such a credit would pay for nearly the full cost of health insurance at very low incomes and phase out as income increases. This is how virtually all proposals for expanded health insurance coverage have operated over the years. The conservative Heritage Foundation, which has pushed for an individual health insurance system for as long as any group, proposed a subsidy system like this in 1989.[11] Governor Mitt Romney and the Democratic Massachusetts legislature agreed on a specific formula in 2006.[12] The Affordable Care Act (ACA) put it into federal law.

The ACA has two related coverage processes. Medicaid, the existing federal and state program for the less fortunate, will cover the very poorest Americans. Under the Affordable Care Act, all nonelderly American citizens and legal residents whose income is at or below 133 percent of the poverty line (roughly $30,000 for a family of four) would become eligible for Medicaid.[13] Because of their particularly low incomes, coverage for this group will be free. As interpreted by the Supreme Court, states can choose to expand coverage in this way or forgo the expansion. Assuming that all states proceed with the expansion, an estimated 17 million people would be added to the program,

TABLE 1

Insurance subsidy in the Affordable Care Act

Income (% of poverty line)	Family payment (% of income)	Typical family payment ($)	Typical subsidy ($)
133–150	3–4	1,100	13,900
150–200	4–6.3	2,200	12,800
200–250	6.3–8.05	3,600	11,400
250–300	8.05–9.5	5,200	9,800
300–400	9.5	7,400	7,600

NOTE: The poverty line is about $22,000 for a family of four. The examples assume a family insurance premium of $15,000, roughly the current national average. The estimates of family payments and subsidy amounts are approximately at the midpoint of the income range.

on top of the approximately 35 million nonelderly people expected to be covered without reform.[14]

The other coverage process applies to families with incomes above 133 percent of the poverty line that do not have employer-based health insurance. These families will receive sliding scale tax credits to purchase insurance. Table 1 shows the amount that families would pay and the corresponding subsidy. The lowest-income families—those earning between 1.33 and 1.5 times the poverty line—would pay 3 to 4 percent of their income for coverage, or about $1,100. This share increases to 9.5 percent of income for families earning up to four times the poverty line (an income of about $88,000). A family at four times the poverty line would pay about $8,400 for insurance and receive a subsidy of about $6,600. Above 400 percent of poverty, there would be no subsidy for health insurance.[15]

People would receive these subsidies to buy insurance through an exchange—an online brokerage for health insurance run by state or federal governments. In 2016, the exchanges are expected to process insurance for 21 million people.[16]

As noted earlier, this system is not hard to design. Versions of such a scheme have been floating around for years. The major issue with the program is funding.[17] The median family in the United States earns $50,000 annually, roughly 250 percent of the poverty line.[18] Thus credits would be available to individuals well into the upper half of the income distribution. This is expensive.

Table 2 shows the financial consequences of this commitment for the federal government. The coverage provisions of the Affordable Care Act take effect in 2014. To avoid phase-in effects, I show the costs in 2016. The left-hand column shows the money spent under the Affordable Care Act in 2016 and the right-hand column shows the funds used to pay for the outlays. There is a slight excess of spending over revenues, but not by a great deal. In 2016, the cost of the Medicaid expansion is estimated to be $81 billion, and the premium subsidies account for another $77 billion. There is an $8 billion cost for additional coverage in the drug program for seniors and small-business health insurance tax credits. The total is $166 billion of new commitments.

To put these numbers in perspective, the Medicare program is expected to spend about $700 billion that year, and federal Medicaid spending (without the coverage expansions) would be about $300 billion. In the overall scale of federal commitments, the coverage provisions amount to about 4 percent of federal government spending.[19]

There are ways of offsetting these costs, and the Affordable Care Act employs many of them. High-income families can afford to pay for some of these expenses. Accordingly, the Act

TABLE 2

Budgetary impact of the Affordable Care Act, 2016

Outlays		Sources of funds	
Medicaid expansion	$81 billion	Reduced Medicare, Medicaid, and CHIP payments	$64 billion
Premium subsidies	$77 billion	Provider fees	$15 billion
Other*	$8 billion	Medicare tax	$33 billion
		Other*	$47 billion
Total	$166 billion	Total	$159 billion

SOURCE: Congressional Budget Office, Letter to the Honorable Nancy Pelosi, March 20, 2010, www.cbo.gov/publication/21351. The Medicaid expansion and premium subsidies are in table 4. Other outlays and sources of funds come from table 2. Reduced Medicare, Medicaid, and CHIP is before the cost of filling in the donut hole. The estimate of other sources is a combination of "Penalty Payments by Employers and Uninsured Individuals," "Associated Effects of Coverage Provisions on Revenues," and "Other Revenue Provisions" from table 2 as well as $10 billion from the CLASS Act.

* Other outlays include filling in the Medicare Part D "donut hole" ($5 billion) and small-employer tax credits ($3 billion). Other sources of funds include penalty payments by employers and uninsured individuals, revenues from the CLASS long-term disability act, miscellaneous impacts of coverage provisions on revenues, and other miscellaneous revenue provisions.

increases the Medicare Hospital Insurance tax on very high earners—a change that will generate $33 billion in revenue in 2016. Further, it increases the estimates of productivity growth expected in the hospital industry (thus justifying less rapid payment increases), reduces overpayments to private plans that enroll Medicare beneficiaries, and makes various other changes to reduce spending on existing public health programs. All told, this yields $159 billion in 2016. The net amount is enough to offset the costs of additional coverage. The Affordable Care Act is thus paid for.

But savings of this magnitude are not easy to obtain. Lowering Medicare payments without similar changes by private insurers will create a fee differential between Medicare and private insurance that would, over time, cause providers to leave the Medicare program. We have seen exactly this effect in Medicaid, where most providers will not accept enrollees who are in the program because payment rates are so low.[20]

Nor does paying the bill once end the problem. The trouble with coverage costs is that they increase over time more rapidly than the revenues used to pay for them. Tax revenue rises with output, roughly at the rate of gross domestic product (GDP) growth. Historically, medical care costs have increased about 1.5 to 2.0 percentage points more rapidly than GDP.[21] When spending rises more rapidly than revenues, programs become unsustainable. Absent other policies, Medicare, Medicaid, and exchange subsidies would soon outstrip our financing ability.

Figure 1 shows this situation. It is estimated that without a change in the rate of increase in medical care costs, the entirety of federal revenues would go to support health care and Social Security by the middle of this century, with no money left for defense, environmental programs, education, interest on the debt, or the myriad other activities of the federal government. The vast bulk of this dire scenario is attributable to rising health care costs.

Of course, these costs need to be weighed against the benefits of covering everybody. Medical care is so expensive and so necessary for a fulfilling life that universal health insurance coverage is clearly the right step. My point is not that coverage is unaffordable or even that it will become unaffordable; rather, the

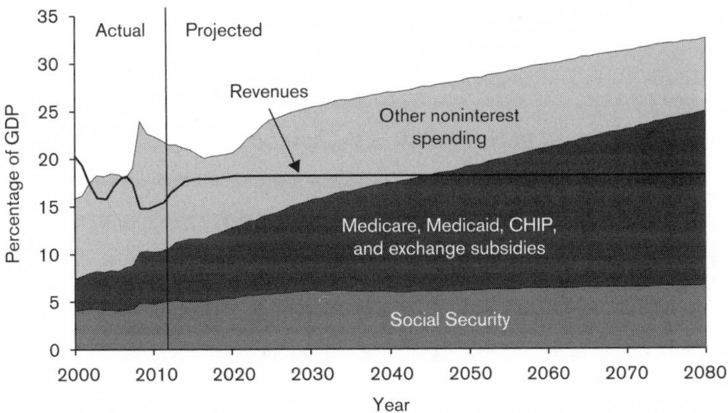

Figure 1. Forecast of the U.S. budget. Tax rates are assumed to be constant, hence revenues as a share of GDP are constant after recovery from the recession. Chart based on the extended baseline scenario of the Congressional Budget Office, *CBO's 2012 Long-Term Budget Outlook* (Washington, DC: Congressional Budget Office, 2012), www.cbo.gov/publication/43288.

point is simply that addressing the access gap is not enough. We will be able to maintain our commitment to universal coverage only if we can solve the cost part of the equation.

• • •

Concern about access involves more than just whether a person has insurance coverage today; it incorporates how insurers will make pricing and coverage decisions in the future. For insurance companies, covering the healthy is much more profitable than covering the sick. When paid the same amount for everyone, the smart insurer will always choose to cover people who use less care; for the same money coming in, less goes out. The consequence is an unfortunate dynamic: insurance companies roll out the red carpet for the healthy but dump the sick. The minute a healthy person becomes ill, the carpet disappears, and the person is encouraged to go elsewhere.

Of course, no one wants to be insured only when healthy. The whole point of insurance is to be secure when illness arises. Thus, the hot potato game of passing off the sick is as inefficient as it is unsettling. In economic parlance, this process is termed "risk selection," and it is one of the pathologies of insurance markets.

This same dynamic explains why people find it hard to identify good insurance plans, even when they are in good health. Insurers do not reach out to people readily, like sellers of other goods. Rather, they wait in reserve, checking whether the person is profitable to insure before offering a policy. Their mentality is: don't encourage people to sign up for insurance unless you know they are healthy. This makes it difficult to comparison shop.

Addressing the insurance runaround is straightforward—at least conceptually. We can simply order insurance companies not to deny coverage to the sick. By requiring that insurers cover the sick on equal terms with the healthy, we can prevent people from being tossed aside when they need care. Further, we can require insurers to post their rates for all to see and allow people to choose freely among different insurers.

The most popular parts of the Affordable Care Act do exactly this. They require insurers to take all comers (termed "guaranteed issue"), prohibit rescinding coverage when people get sick ("guaranteed renewability"), limit premium variation between the healthy and sick ("modified community rating"), and ban lifetime limits on coverage. The law further requires states or the federal government to set up an online insurance exchange allowing people simpler access to insurance. Plans that want to sell to people would apply to the exchange, with rates essentially the same for all.[22] None of this is novel. It builds off regulations that many states have already enacted and enforce.[23] Even insurance companies were not surprised to see these regulations.

But there is a catch: implementing these regulations can have unintended consequences. Allowing sick people to get coverage whenever they want invites healthy people to postpone obtaining coverage until they really need it. Why buy coverage when you are not in need, if you can get it the moment you fall sick? If the healthy people drop out of the market, however, the rates for the rest must rise; no insurer can cover the average price of the most expensive people while charging premiums that are below their cost. When rates rise, this encourages still more people—the healthiest of the remainder—to drop out as well. The net effect is a "death spiral"—fewer and fewer people covered at higher and higher prices.[24] Without a mechanism to stop this dynamic, regulation creates severe problems.

The only way to make insurance regulations work is to ensure that almost all people are covered almost all of the time—in sickness and in health. Some economists assert that insurance regulations should not even be attempted unless healthy people are required to buy coverage. The Obama Justice Department took this view when the U.S. Supreme Court was considering the constitutionality of the requirement to buy coverage in the Affordable Care Act.[25] It suggested to the court that if it struck down the requirement that all individuals buy health insurance, it also needed to strike down the regulations that require insurers to sell to everyone on a fair basis. Others believe the situation is not so dire, that with generous subsidies we can prevent the insurance market from unraveling. In the end, the Supreme Court upheld the requirement that all individuals buy coverage, so the issue of whether the insurance regulations needed to be struck down was moot.

What all agree on is that for regulation of insurance coverage to be successful, insurance must be generally affordable. Thus insurance reform directly links to the issue of premium subsidies; we can't attempt one without the other. And that brings us back to the costs of those subsidies.

• • •

In health care, all roads lead to costs. And those costs are big numbers. The average American spends $8,000 annually on medical care—including the amount individuals pay out of pocket, the amount that insurers (or employers) pay for them, and the amount that governments collect as taxes to support public health care programs.[26] As Figure 2 shows, this is over twice the average of other rich countries.

Since the United States is richer than other countries, it ought to spend more on medical care. But income alone does not explain these differences. Even as a share of income, medical spending in the United States is 50 percent higher than in other countries.

Medical care used to be much less expensive. In 1960, medical spending per person was about $900 (adjusted for inflation)—only one-tenth as much as today. As Figure 3 shows, in 1960, U.S. spending as a share of GDP was relatively comparable to spending in other countries (only 10 percent higher). In the past five decades, spending on medical care in the United States has exceeded the growth of the economy by nearly 2 percentage points annually. While growth in medical spending has exceeded GDP growth in all countries, the gap has been larger in the United States than elsewhere. The result is a growing

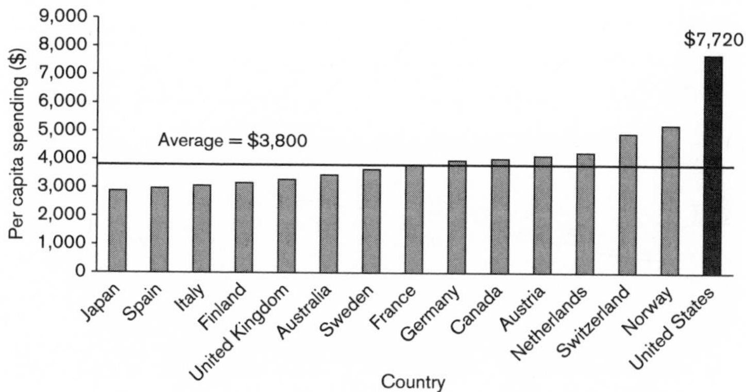

Figure 2. Medical spending in high-income countries, 2009. Data collected by the Organization for Economic Co-operation and Development, *Health at a Glance 2011: OECD Indicators* (2011), table 7.1.1, www.oecd.org/health/health-systems/49105858.pdf.

divergence in spending between the United States and similarly rich countries; the gap in 2007 was 55 percent.

Most estimates suggest that this differential between medical spending increases and GDP increases will continue over time. The Congressional Budget Office and the actuaries at the Department of Health and Human Services believe that growth in health care costs will exceed income growth by 1 percent or more for the indefinite future.[27]

Notice the emphasis on total medical spending, not just Medicare or Medicaid. Costs for both public and private medical care programs are rising over time, at approximately the same rate. The United States has a problem with medical care costs, not solely a problem with government program costs.

The consequences of growth in spending on medical care exceeding the growth of the economy are profound. Tax reve-

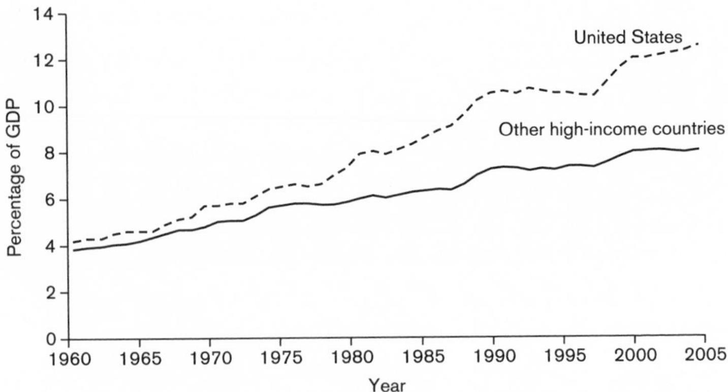

Figure 3. Acute medical spending as a share of GDP, 1960–2008. Data are from the Organization for Economic Co-operation and Development, *Health at a Glance 2011: OECD Indicators* (2011), table 7.1.1, www.oecd.org/health/health-systems/49105858.pdf. "Other high-income countries" include those in figure 2. Because of differences in the treatment of the residential component of long-term care services, data are presented for acute care services only—generally hospitals, physicians, and prescription drugs. Some countries changed the methodology for estimating medical spending in various years. These breaks in the data were adjusted for by increasing or decreasing spending in the year prior to the break, assuming that spending in the year of the break grew by the average of the year before and the year after the break. See David M. Cutler and Dan Ly, "The (Paper)Work of Medicine: Understanding International Medical Costs," *Journal of Economic Perspectives* 25, no. 2 (2011): 3–25, www.aeaweb.org/articles.php?doi = 10.1257/jep.25.2.3.

nue rises with the growth of the economy. If medical costs increase more rapidly than economic growth, it means there is a growing burden on the government. The burden is more acute in recessions than in expansions, but it never disappears. At the business level, sales for the typical firm are increasing approximately with the growth of the economy. Thus, when medical care increases more rapidly than GDP, employers encounter financing difficulties with their health plans. Almost always, these costs are passed back to workers, whose cash wages increase less rapidly than their productivity.[28]

Families then feel the squeeze of rising medical costs from all directions: higher costs for health insurance, increased copays at the doctor's office, smaller increases in take-home pay, and tax dollars that increasingly go to health care and away from education, public works, environmental protection, and other areas.

The major issue is whether this spending is worth it. Is the money we increasingly put into medical care valuable or not? And if the money is not worth it, how do we do better? The value proposition, as economists term it, is the most important question in all of medical care. I turn to it next.

CHAPTER TWO

The Value Proposition

Where does all the medical spending go? The common perception is that high spending involves excessive profits for insurance and pharmaceutical companies, high advertising and marketing expenses, and outlandish pay for health care CEOs. In a survey conducted by the Consumers Union, 76 percent of participants cited pharmaceutical companies as the reasons for high costs, and 77 percent cited insurance companies. Only 59 and 47 percent named hospitals and doctors, respectively.[1]

In this case, people's perceptions are wrong. Figure 4 shows that pharmaceutical spending in total accounts for only 10 percent of medical spending, and insurance company administrative costs for only 7 percent. Far more important are hospital costs (33 percent) and professional services (28 percent), which include physicians and dentists.

If excessive profits were the cause of high spending, the solution to the health care cost problem would be easy. Advertising, marketing, and CEO pay can be regulated and reduced. Sadly, however, we need to go to the primary areas of health care utili-

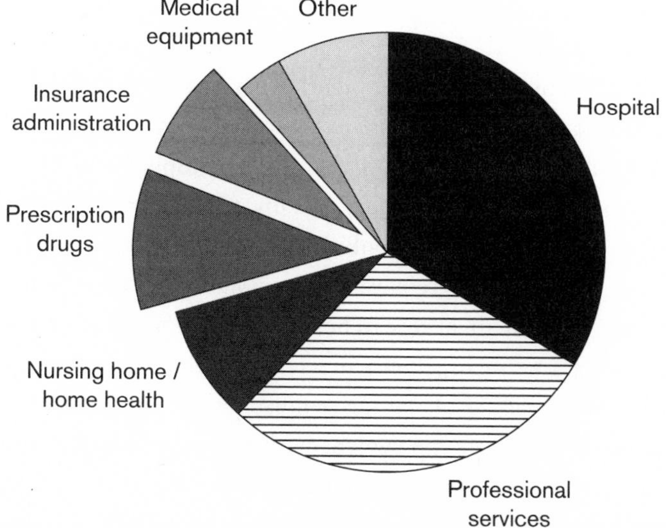

Figure 4. Distribution of medical spending, 2011. Data compiled by the Center for Medicare and Medicaid Services, *National Health Expenditure Accounts,* www.cms.gov/Research-Statistics-Data-and-Systems/Statistics-Trends-and-Reports/NationalHealthExpendData/Downloads/tables.pdf.

zation—doctor and hospital visits for the sick. Changing these aspects of the medical system is hard.

The level of spending reflects medical care use, and so too does the growth in spending. While insurance administrative costs and prescription drug spending have increased over time, they have done so at approximately the same pace as hospital and physician costs. All health care is more expensive than it used to be, regardless of the source.

Why, then, have costs increased? The fundamental fact about the medical system is that over time it has become significantly more advanced in its ability to treat the sick. Consider two examples from different areas of medicine: heart disease and premature infants.[2] In 1960, when medical spending in the United States was a bit more than one-tenth what it is today, treatment of heart disease was not extensive. Standard treatment for a heart attack consisted of bed rest—six weeks in a hospital bed, followed by six months at home. Surgery was uncommon, and even medications that are used commonly today—drugs that lower cholesterol or reduce blood pressure, for example—were unavailable.

Over time, medical researchers have developed new ways to treat heart disease, especially in its more serious manifestations. Diagnostic imaging of the heart muscle and coronary arteries permits surgeons to experiment with new open-heart surgical techniques. These techniques can reroute blood flow around occluded arteries (coronary artery bypass grafting), or reopen arteries that have narrowed (angioplasty, often with stent insertion). Coronary care units specialize in monitoring the care of such patients. And new, high-cost medications reduce disease onset and recurrence. The result has been an explosion in medical spending. Treatment in the aftermath of a heart attack jumped from very cheap to an average of $30,000 per person.

The same pattern is apparent in care for premature infants. In 1960, such care was essentially nonexistent, and many premature infants died shortly after birth as a result of underdeveloped breathing capacity. Today, these infants are treated in specialized neonatal intensive care units, where they may receive synthetic surfactant to open their tiny lung sacs, operations to repair congenital anomalies, and medication and monitoring to prevent infections. Again, this is expensive. The typical premature infant receives nearly $50,000 of medical care in the first year of life.[3] Furthermore, there may be later costs to address complications from being born prematurely.

Spending more on people who are sick (often) brings health improvements. This is true for both cardiovascular disease and low-birth-weight infants. The mortality rate from cardiovascular disease has declined by more than 50 percent since 1950, at least partly because of this additional spending. Similarly, the mortality rate for the smallest infants fell by 50 percent between 1950 and today.

These survival improvements are worth a lot. In a society that has most of life's necessities, people highly value their health. We pay for safety devices that might never be needed, demand additional money to work in dangerous jobs, and support government programs to reduce chemical risks—even when they drive up the price of goods. By parsing the various decisions people make, economists have been able to estimate how much people are willing to pay to extend the life of a typical person. To make the estimates comparable across age groups, the "value of life" (as it is termed) is often expressed per year. What are people willing to give up for an extra year of life? Across a wide range of studies, a general estimate is that a year of life in good health is worth about $100,000, with a range of $50,000 to $200,000.[4]

At these valuations, the benefit of medical advancement is significantly greater than the cost. Reducing low-birth-weight mortality adds about seventy years of life for many infants. People who are saved from heart attack death live for less time but still a good while—generally about five years. The cost is high, but so are the benefits.

Indeed, the benefits are so large that they generally swamp the costs. Between 1960 and 2000, life expectancy has increased by about five years because cardiovascular disease mortality has declined. An economic valuation of this additional longevity is about $500,000. This is significantly greater than the additional

$30,000 spent treating each heart attack. Indeed, when economists do direct calculations of the costs and benefits of medical advance, they generally conclude that the benefits of this care are five to ten times the cost of the care.

Individuals have not done this calculation on their own, but many sense the results. When people are asked whether they want to address Medicare cost problems by cutting Medicare spending or raising taxes, they generally prefer to raise taxes.[5]

• • •

If medical spending is so valuable, why is it commonly believed that there is a cost problem? The problem is not that all cost growth is excessive, but rather that some spending is unnecessary, and this unnecessary part is a large amount of money. The United States spends about $2.5 trillion annually on medical care. The best guess of health economists is that about one-third of this total—nearly $1 trillion annually—is not associated with improved outcomes. That is, we could eliminate about $1 trillion in spending per year and still have better health. At the individual level, that works out to over $2,000 per person per year.

One way to see the magnitude of excessive spending is by comparing the international data presented in the previous chapter. As noted there, the United States spends more than other countries on medical care. But the value of this additional spending appears to be limited. Health outcomes are no better in the United States than elsewhere—even for patients who suffer a heart attack or have other acute diseases.[6] This is in marked contrast to the increase in spending over time, where spending is associated with significantly better health.

The difference between spending growth over time and spending differences across countries is important. Over time, there is a lot more technology available in medical care than there used to be. But at a given point in time, the knowledge about what can be done is similar across countries. Thus, the difference internationally is not what can be done (with the exception of very poor countries, where access to technology is a real constraint), but how much the technology is used and how much is paid for it. By comparison with other countries, the United States uses technology in lower-value settings and pays more for the same care.

Let me be more formal. A number of recent studies have looked in detail at the efficiency with which medical care is delivered in the United States. This includes studies from the Institute of Medicine, the former head of the Medicare and Medicaid programs, and influential outside research groups.[7] The short version of their conclusions is shown in table 3. Excessive costs are found in six areas:

Unnecessary Services. Unnecessary services are those services that do not need to be provided but are done anyway. Nearly $200 billion is spent annually on overused medical services.

The poster child for overused care is treatment of back pain. Lower back pain is one of the most common and costly medical conditions in the country. Eight out of ten Americans will experience lower back pain in their lifetime,[8] and 15 to 20 percent will experience it in any given year. In 2005 alone, total spending on spine care was $86 billion.[9] The care provided ranges from relatively inexpensive (muscle relaxants, analgesics) to very expensive (MRIs and spine surgery).

Back pain can be differentiated into simple and complex cases. Simple back pain is limited in scope, while more serious pain typically manifests itself also in other parts of the body, including leg pain, fever, and dysfunctional excretion. Optimal

TABLE 3
Excessive Medicare spending

Area	Examples	Cost (in $U.S. billions)	% of total spending
Poor care delivery			
Unnecessary services	Back surgeries, elective inductions, stenting	192	7
Failures of care delivery	Medical errors	128	5
Failures of care coordination	Inadequate risk factor control, poor use of chronic medications, hospital readmissions	35	1
Excessive admin. costs	Billing and insurance-related services	248	9
Inflated prices	MRI prices	131	5
Fraud/abuse	Home health care fraud	177	7
Total		910	34

SOURCE: Donald M. Berwick and Andrew D. Hackbarth, "Eliminating Waste in U.S. Health Care," *Journal of the American Medical Association* (2012): E1–E4, http://jama.jamanetwork.com/article.aspx?articleid=1148376. The table shows midrange estimates of excessive medical care spending.

treatment differs for simple and complex back pain. Surgery is generally not necessary if pain is due to something minor, such as a pulled muscle. In this case, physical therapy is more helpful—and considerably cheaper.[10] MRIs, spine surgery, and the like are generally necessary and appropriate only in more complex cases.

Despite the evidence that back surgery is often not needed for simple cases, simple back pain is typically treated far more intensively than clinical conditions warrant. Spine surgeries are

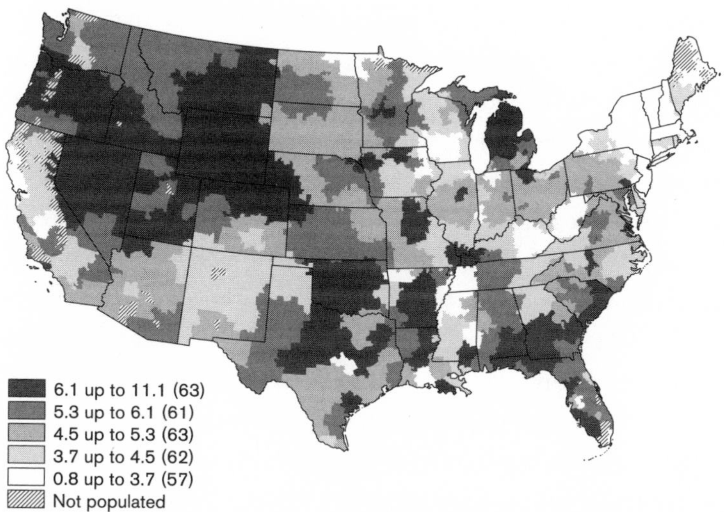

Figure 5. Back surgeries per 1,000 Medicare enrollees, 2010. Rates of back surgery range from approximately 2 operations per 1,000 beneficiaries to over 6 operations per 1,000 beneficiaries. This variation is not associated with patient need. Figures in parentheses indicate the number of hospital referral regions in each category. Kristin Bronner at Dartmouth helpfully provided the chart, based on unpublished data.

conducted twice as frequently in the United States as they are in other countries, and rates of surgery here have been increasing over time.[11] The back surgery operation rate also differs markedly across areas in the United States. Figure 5 shows that for Medicare beneficiaries, the rate of back surgery is highest in the Pacific Northwest, the upper Midwest, and parts of the South (Alabama in particular) and lowest in New England. The difference between high- and low-use areas is a factor of six to one.

This variation in surgery rates is not due to need. Studies show that only one-tenth of the geographic variation in surgery is due to the nature of the patient population.[12] Rather, the differences are the outcome of haphazard processes. Primary care physicians manage some people with back pain, while others are referred to orthopedists, who more commonly order MRIs and recommend back surgery.[13]

A second example of overuse is elective induction of preterm birth. The medical literature is clear that elective induction of labor should be performed only on women who are at over thirty-nine weeks of gestation;[14] the consequences of earlier induction include higher rates of cesarean sections and increased use of the neonatal intensive care unit by the newborn baby.[15] Unfortunately, early induction of labor is routine. As many as 40 percent of inductions are performed before thirty-nine weeks of gestation.[16] Many factors contribute to this overuse: convenience for the mother or doctor and a desire to have the birth with a trusted physician are some explanations. Almost certainly, women undergoing preterm induced labor are unaware of the risks of the decision; for many doctors, the risks are not a pressing concern.

A third example of unnecessary care is excessive use of stenting (formally termed percutaneous coronary intervention, or PCI). Coronary stents are often used when the arteries supplying blood to the heart become occluded; the stent, when combined with balloon angioplasty, keeps the artery wall open. Over one million stents were inserted in 2004.[17]

Some stent insertions are clearly valuable.[18] Studies show a reduction in mortality associated with stenting in the immediate aftermath of a heart attack.[19] Use in other circumstances is less clear, however. Many people have mild chest pain or have had a heart attack in the past, and physicians fear there could be a new coronary event in the future. Is prophylactic stenting helpful for such patients? A number of clinical studies have attempted to determine the value of stent insertion in such cases. Despite the general belief that stent insertion should be helpful, the studies generally conclude otherwise.

Research published in 2006 and 2007 found that stenting was no more effective than medical therapy in preventing death or future heart attacks for people with stable coronary disease (*stable* is defined as disease that occurs during exertion and resolves at rest).[20] Many cardiologists acknowledged these studies but still held the belief that stenting improved quality of life. Alas, that turned out to be untrue also. A study published in 2008 found that stenting did not have a significant positive effect on quality of life either.[21]

Despite these results, stent insertion is still common, even in patients with stable coronary disease. As many as 85 percent of stents are given to patients with stable disease, at a cost of about $15,000 per stent (including surgical and hospital fees).[22]

These examples of unnecessary care highlight a central fact about waste in medical care. It is not that entire classes of care are unnecessary or inappropriate. Spinal surgery, induced labor, and stent insertion are all extremely valuable services when performed on the right patients. Rather, the point is that care is appropriate in some cases but inappropriate in others, and the medical system does a poor job of separating appropriate use from inappropriate use. To use an analogy, health care waste is like fat layered into beef. One cannot remove it by simply cutting entire slabs. Rather, a delicate and deft knife is needed to separate the good from the bad.

Inefficiently Delivered Services. Inefficiently delivered services represent misuse of the health care system. They include services during which errors are made or where poor infrastructure means that care is delivered incorrectly.

Hospital-acquired infections (HAIs), or infections acquired during medical care for another illness, are a primary example of inefficient care delivery. It is estimated that about 4.5 HAIs occur for every hundred patients admitted to the hospital. In 2002, nearly 99,000 people died of an HAI. Estimates suggest that HAIs cost about $40 billion annually.[23]

A classic example of an HAI is a bloodstream infection associated with a central line, known as a CLABSI. A central line is a small catheter inserted into a vein in the neck, chest, or groin to monitor the blood, inject medication, or provide nutrition. It provides easy access to the bloodstream in patients who need repeated injections or whose veins are hard to locate. But a central line that is not inserted using sterile procedures or is not changed regularly may induce infection. Without proper precautions, environmental bacteria—from the nurse's or doctor's hands or a nearby surface—can contaminate the catheter or needle before it enters the vein, allowing bacteria to enter the bloodstream.[24] Bloodstream infections are serious and may result in death or a prolonged hospital stay.

There are protocols that medical personnel can follow to essentially eliminate such infections.[25] Peter Pronovost of Johns Hopkins University has pioneered the use of these protocols and has demonstrated that institutions can use them to essentially eliminate infections.[26] The protocols basically involve standardizing safe hygienic practice: ensuring that providers wash their hands, making sure the area is sterile, and changing catheters and other instruments frequently. Still, use of the guidelines remains low. The CDC estimates that if the Pronovost protocols were universally followed and CLABSIs were eliminated, the savings would be up to $9 billion annually.[27]

In most areas of American industry, error rates have been substantially reduced. To give an example, the accident rate for Western-built airplanes (the number of hulls destroyed in every one million flights) fell 42 percent from 2001 to 2010. The likelihood of an accident is now one in every 1.6 million flights;[28] the death rate from medical errors, by contrast, is the equivalent of a medium-sized jumbo jet crashing daily.

Of course, health care is different from flying a plane or manufacturing a car. Pilots fly the same route regularly, and manufacturers typically make one product for a lengthy period of time before switching to another. In health care, however, the product must be tailored to each customer. Thus some degree of error is natural.

But the power of this excuse is limited. While individuals make mistakes, good systems catch those mistakes before they turn fatal. This is the whole point of the checklist for inserting central lines. Let's go back to the reduction in airline fatalities. In his book *Outliers,* Malcolm Gladwell discusses how airlines reduced accidents, focusing specifically on Korean Air's fatal 1997 crash in Guam.[29] Korean Air Flight 801 was too close to the ground before it landed, and as a result, the plane crashed into a hill. Two hundred and twenty-eight passengers died. While there were many causes of the crash, inefficient communication between crew members was clearly one.[30] The first officer and the flight engineer observed that Flight 801 was too close to the ground, but their attempts to alert the pilot were not forceful enough, and their warnings were not heeded. Even the computerized Ground Proximity Warning System was ignored.[31]

Consideration of flight deck culture shows why this was the case. The Korean Air flight deck was very hierarchical. The pilot was in charge, and everyone else deferred to him. In the flight in question, this obedience was critical to the outcome. Without a team culture on the flight deck, the plane crashed.

Health care is like the Korean Airlines example. Doctors are in charge, and everyone else is subordinate. In such a situation, mistakes can have grave outcomes.[32] But while airlines have adopted a systemwide approach to improving quality, health care has not. Whereas complete obedience to the pilot is no longer encouraged, total deference to a senior surgeon still is. This explains why airline crashes have fallen dramatically, while health care mistakes have been virtually unchanged. The result is a major health and financial loss.

Missed Prevention Opportunities. Missed prevention is underuse of the health care system. By providing the right care earlier on, we can improve health and often save money down the road.

There are three types of prevention: primary, secondary, and tertiary. Primary prevention refers to stopping disease before it occurs; smoking cessation is one example. Secondary prevention involves preventing chronic disease from becoming acute. A patient who has high blood pressure can reduce the probability of a stroke by taking medication to treat blood pressure. Tertiary prevention involves keeping acute disease under control. A patient who has congestive heart failure may have missed opportunities for primary and secondary prevention; however, he or she can still benefit from tertiary prevention.

Tertiary prevention has the clearest cost savings. About 20 percent of Medicare beneficiaries who are discharged from a hospital are readmitted within one month for a very similar condition.[33] Often the patient did not see a doctor or nurse in the intervening period, and many did not take medications appropriately. Preventing readmission is not difficult. Ensuring understanding of medication recommendations and adherence to them, as well as seeing a physician or nurse after discharge, can prevent many readmissions. Many organizations around the country have figured out how to do this and have very low rates of readmission as a result.[34] The savings from emulating this nationally would be large. Estimates suggest that about half of the $28 billion Medicare spends annually on readmissions could be saved through known interventions, and three times that amount could be saved by bringing readmissions down to the levels of the best systems.[35]

The financial savings from primary and secondary prevention are more speculative, because there are significant costs and the benefits are diffuse. For example, smoking cessation costs money (nicotine replacement therapy, for example) and may lead to higher medical costs down the road (smokers rarely live long enough to need long-term nursing home care). But some studies do suggest possible savings from primary and secondary prevention.[36]

Excessive Administrative Costs. Administrative costs consist of time and effort spent on the paperwork of health care—including billing, referrals, and credentialing. A massive infrastructure supports these administrative tasks. There are 2.2 administrative workers for every office-based physician, and there are 1.5 administrative workers for every hospital bed.[37] All told, 14 percent of all U.S. health care expenditures are for administrative expenses.[38] This is twice the amount spent on heart disease and three times the spending on cancer.

There is no doubt that this total can be reduced. The Institute of Medicine estimates that administrative costs could be cut by nearly $250 billion annually with no adverse consequences—

Figure 6. Administrative complexity through the provider revenue cycle.

indeed, quality of life for patients and physicians would improve.[39]

What are all these administrative personnel doing? Figure 6 shows a high-level typology of administrative costs.[40] One part is credentialing. The average physician submits eighteen credentialing applications annually (each insurer, hospital, ambulatory surgery facility, and so on requires a different one), consuming seventy minutes of staff time and eleven minutes of physician time per application. Verifying eligibility for services is also costly. Insurance information must be verified for twenty to thirty patients daily, including three to four patients for whom verification must be sought orally. Because people change insurance plans frequently, and the cost sharing they are charged varies with the plan and past utilization (e.g., how much of the deductible have they spent?), the determination of what to charge a patient is especially difficult. Because of lags in claims reporting, providers often have to collect additional money from patients after the fact.

Finally, significant time is spent on billing and payment collection.[41] On average, about three claims are denied per physician per week and need to be rebilled. Often claims are denied because additional documentation is required (which cannot be supplied electronically due to outdated computer systems), or because coverage status is uncertain. Three-quarters of denied bills are ultimately paid, but the administrative cost of securing payment is high. Indeed, the administrative burden has risen as insurance policies have become more complex, while the technology of administration has not kept pace.

The administrative burden differs by payer. Medicare imposes low administrative costs, as do most government-run systems in other countries; there is no utilization review or preauthorization requirement for Medicare-covered services. Billing is also straightforward. Private insurers impose higher administrative costs but also pay more generously.

Prices That Are Too High. Prices for the same medical service vary enormously across providers. Figure 7 shows one example: the price of abdominal CT scans at different Massachusetts hospitals in 2009. The highest-paid hospital receives nearly four times more for an abdominal CT than the lowest-paid hospital. Since an abdominal CT is relatively straightforward, this price difference does not reflect important dimensions of quality. Rather, it reflects market power. The hospitals charging more are the most prestigious ones (Children's Hospital, Massachusetts General Hospital), and the ones charging the least are the less-esteemed facilities. In a series of reports, the attorney general of Massachusetts has shown that big health care providers command tremendous market power, translating into high overall spending and rapid spending growth.[42]

Building on this, estimates suggest that national medical spending could be reduced by about 4 percent—or over $100 billion annually—if prices were lowered to competitive levels.[43]

Fraud. Medical fraud costs the United States billions of dollars every year.[44] Much of this fraud is directed against government insurance programs, though some also occurs in

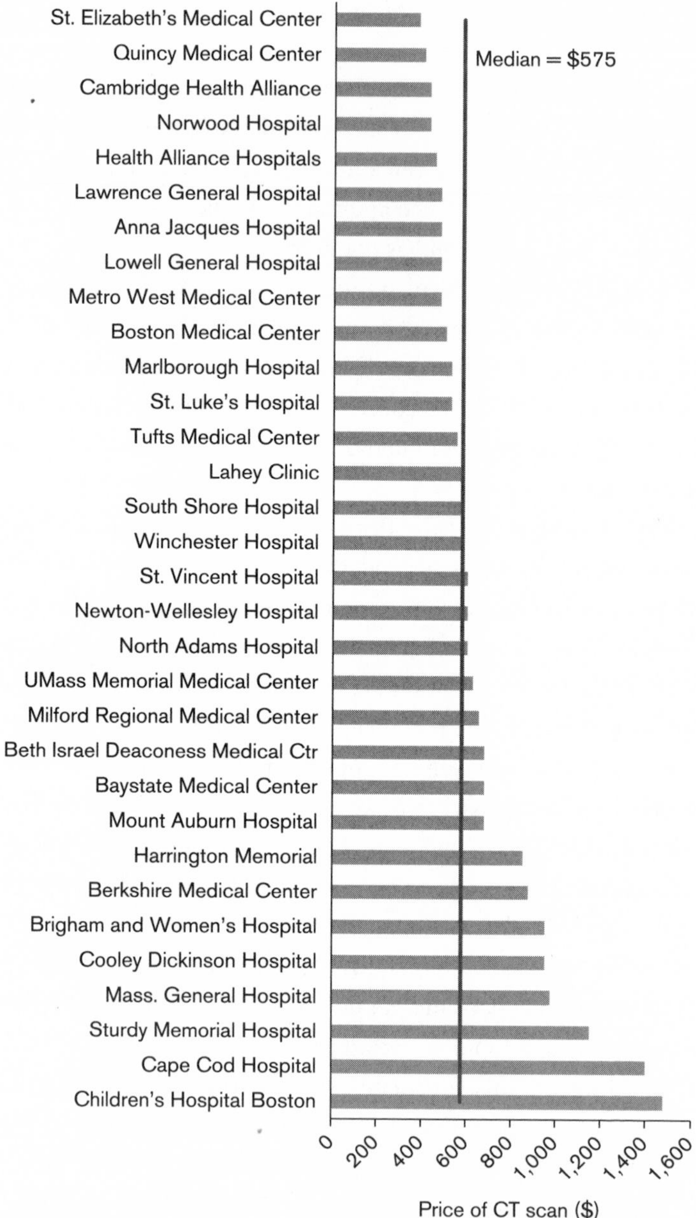

Figure 7. Price of an abdominal CT scan in Massachusetts hospitals, 2010. Data compiled by Massachusetts Association of Health Plans, *2011 Annual Report* (Boston, MA: MAHP, 2011), www.mahp.com/assets/pdfs/MAHP-Annual-2011-Annual-Report.pdf.

private insurance. One investigation revealed that providers in Miami-Dade County in Florida were overreporting their Medicare expenditures for durable medical equipment and home health in order to get greater reimbursements.[45] Two home health providers, ABC Home Health Care and Florida Home Health Care, billed Medicare for $25 million of unnecessary or fabricated services. On January 5, 2012, three employees of Florida Home Health and ABC were sentenced to prison.[46] All told, about 3 percent of medical care spending is estimated to be fraudulent, although this estimate is uncertain.

• • •

Four of the six categories in table 3 are associated with poor provision of medical services (the exceptions are administrative costs and fraud)—either too much care, too little, or care from the wrong providers or in the wrong settings. It is useful to know more about this misallocation of resources.

The basics of these mistakes can be seen in figure 8. Most people start off life (at birth or at the onset of adulthood) in relatively good health. As people age, they often acquire chronic conditions. When those conditions are not managed well, the situation becomes serious, requiring acute and postacute care.

People receive many kinds of care from a number of different providers. Primary care physicians are a source of much routine care, and specialists handle particular diseases. There are also hospitals, pharmaceutical companies, labs, nursing homes, home health agencies, durable medical equipment suppliers, and hospices. Although people often need many of these services to treat a particular condition, these providers are by and large in separate physical settings and operate under separate organizational entities. This is part of the problem.

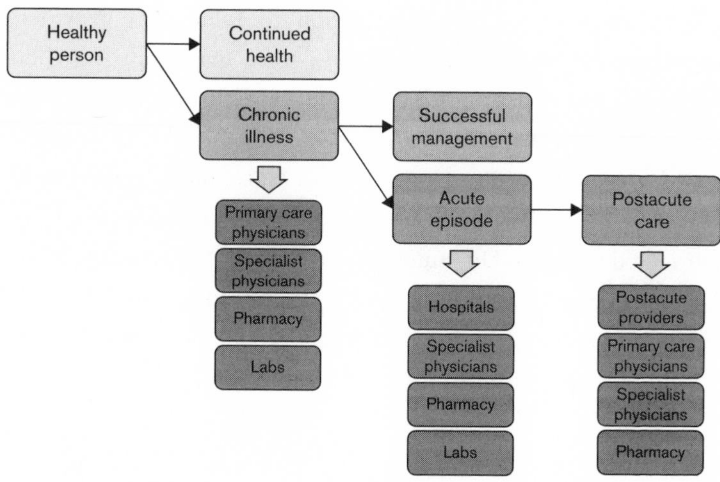

Figure 8. The progression of health and medical care. This figure shows how health progresses and when patients use medical care.

In figure 8, poor prevention is illustrated by transitions from healthy states to less healthy states that are more frequent than is appropriate. Uncoordinated care is defined as substandard management of patients given their health state.

Figure 8 also serves to characterize where the money goes in medical care. Spending on people who are very sick—the acute and postacute care noted in the figure—constitutes the vast bulk of medical care. In the Medicare program, for example, half of medical spending is related to a hospitalization within the previous six months.[47] Essentially all the rest is used to detect and treat chronic disease; only 2 percent goes for prevention.

The concentration of spending in acute situations explains why spending is as high as it is, even when so many people do not use much care. The top 1 percent of all health care users in a year accounts for 30 percent of the health care dollars, and the next 4 percent use another 30 percent. The bottom 50 percent of the population, in contrast, uses only 3 percent of the total health care resources.[48]

This description of health care waste is depressing. Waste is rampant and seems immune to easy solutions. But difficult problems are not impossible ones. In the next chapter, I examine some answers to the cost problem.

CHAPTER THREE

The Cost Control Debate

"Which country has the best health care system in the world?" It's an easy question to ask but a hard one to answer. Imagine walking into a bar during football season and asking the assembled crowd, "Which team is the best this year?" You would receive a variety of impassioned arguments but probably little agreement.

Economists are foolish, so they spend a good deal of time debating these questions. In 2000, the World Health Organization ranked France first and England eighteenth. The British were mad. Argentina was ranked above Brazil; Brazil responded by trying to eliminate funding for the World Health Organization. The United States was ranked thirty-seventh. All in all, it was not a happy episode.[1]

Getting away from specific countries and evaluating types of systems is more manageable, though opinions are still not uniform. Broadly speaking, there are two dominant views about the best medical care systems: the single-payer advocates and the free marketeers. A summary of the differing beliefs of these two groups is shown in table 4.

TABLE 4
Approaches to cost containment

		Consumer price sensitivity	
Single payer	Payment reform	Insurance choice	Treatment choice
Restrict use to eliminate waste, achieve administrative efficiencies	Incentivize better care from providers and consumers	Give insurers incentives to manage care	Increase cost sharing when using services

The single-payer group is represented predominantly in left-of-center organizations; Physicians for a National Health Program is a leader.[2] Advocates of single-payer health care look around the world and notice a common trend: countries in which government is a bigger part of the medical care system spend less than countries with more private involvement, and their health outcomes do not seem to suffer. In a typical European country, health care paid for by the government averages 76 percent of total spending; in the United States, the comparable share is 48 percent. Thus, for single-payer advocates, more government involvement is the natural solution to health care spending. As Physicians for a National Health Program puts it, "Under the current system, expanding access to health care inevitably means increasing costs, and reducing costs inevitably means limiting access. But an NHI [National Health Insurance] could both expand access and reduce costs."[3]

We saw earlier that the United States spends much more than single-payer countries on medical care. Coupled with this is the finding that health outcomes are no better in the United States than in countries that spend less. Figure 9 shows the relationship

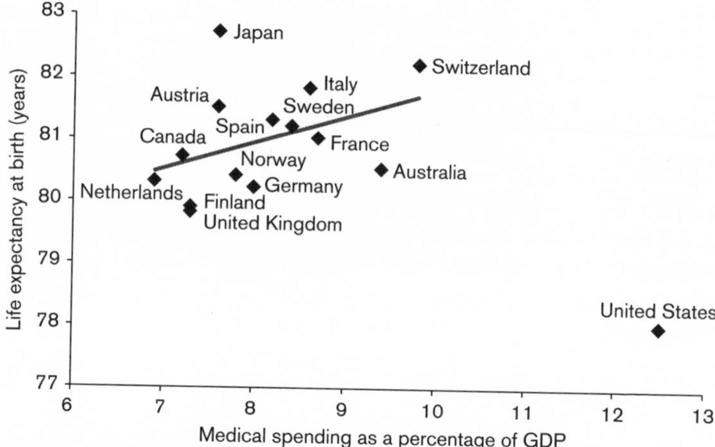

Figure 9. Comparison of life expectancy and medical spending. The regression line was estimated excluding the United States. Data are from the Organization for Economic Cooperation and Development, *Health at a Glance 2011: OECD Indicators* (2011), table 7.1.1, www.oecd.org/health/health-systems/49105858.pdf.

between life expectancy at birth and medical spending as a share of GDP across rich countries. Life expectancy is not an ideal measure of the medical system—many factors other than medical care affect longevity—but it is useful for this purpose. There is a modest upward slope to the line and one big outlier: the United States, where spending is much higher, but outcomes are worse than average.

The important question is how other countries achieve these outcomes. Just having the government pay for more of health care doesn't mean that spending will necessarily be lower. Medicare in the United States is more expensive than Medicare in Canada, for example. How, then, do these countries spend less? For simplicity's sake, I'll refer to the high-government group of countries as "Europe" (objections notwithstanding, I have added Canada and East Asia to "Europe") and contrast Europe with the United States. What do European countries do differently?

There are three major differences between the United States and Europe. First, the United States pays more for the same services compared with other countries. Branded pharmaceutical prices are notoriously higher in the United States than elsewhere,[4] but there is more. The cost of an MRI in Canada, for example, averages about $300; the comparable number in the United States is about $1,000.[5] These lower prices abroad partly explain how countries like Japan can have more MRIs than the United States but spend less than we do.

Physicians' earnings differ even more. The typical specialist physician in the United States earns $230,000 annually (table 5). In Canada, a comparable physician earns $161,000, and in France, the average is $131,000. Only in the Netherlands are specialists paid more than in the United States. Differences in provider incomes account for one-third of the difference in medical spending between the United States and Canada. Further, the United States has a higher share of specialists than do other countries. All told, the United States spends nearly as much more on higher physician earnings as on higher pharmaceutical costs.[6]

We could certainly obtain some medical services, such as pharmaceuticals, more cheaply. But paying doctors less is not so easy. All high-income people in the United States earn more than high-income people in other countries, and thus the pay of physicians is not out of line relative to other highly educated people. For example, the typical specialist in the United States earns 1.37 times what the typical high-income earner makes (i.e., those between the ninety-fifth and the ninety-ninth percentile

TABLE 5

Comparison of physician earnings across countries

Country	Specialists: Average earnings (000s)	Specialists: Ratio of earnings to: GDP per capita	Specialists: Ratio of earnings to: High earners*	General practitioners: ratio to high earners
United States	$230	5.8	1.37	0.92
Australia	$173	5.3	2.54	0.98
Canada	$161	5.0	2.11	1.41
France	$131	4.4	1.47	0.92
Germany	$155	5.4	1.45	1.06
Italy	$84	3.0	1.31	—
Netherlands	$286	8.7	2.56	1.06
New Zealand	$87	3.5	1.47	0.86
Norway	$79	1.9	0.78	0.68
Portugal	$79	4.3	1.11	0.69
Sweden	$71	2.3	0.98	0.86
Switzerland	$130	3.7	0.87	0.77
United Kingdom	$114	3.7	0.80	1.02
Non-U.S. average	$129	4.3	1.45	0.94
Ratio: U.S./non-U.S.	1.78	1.35	0.94	0.98

SOURCE: This chart is taken from my work with Dan Ly and is based on earnings data from the Organization for Economic Co-operation and Development. Data are in 2004 dollars and are adjusted to 2004 as described in the Congressional Research Service. See David M. Cutler and Dan P. Ly, "The (Paper)Work of Medicine: Understanding International Medical Costs," *Journal of Economic Perspectives* 25, no. 2 (2011): 3–25. Data on top earners are from Facundo Alvaredo et al., 2011, *Top Income Database*, Paris School of Economics, http://topincomes.g-mond.parisschoolofeconomics.eu/. Adjustment to 2004 dollars is presented in U.S. Congressional Research Service, *U.S. Health Care Spending: Comparison with Other OECD Countries* (2007).

* High earners are people in the 95th to 99th percentile of the earnings distribution. Primary care and specialist incomes are reported combined for Norway and Portugal and distributed between general practice and specialty based on the differential in Sweden (for Norway) and France (for Portugal).

of the income distribution; see table 5). In European countries, the average is 1.45 times. U.S. specialists are thus slightly *under-paid* by this metric. The same is true for primary care physicians.

Clearly one reason for high medical spending in the United States is that income distribution as a whole is more unequal in the United States, and health care uses many highly skilled workers. There is little the health care system can do about this—though overall income distribution is certainly responsive to policy.

Greater administrative efficiency is a second reason that single-payer countries spend less than the United States. The high spending on administration in the United States, noted previously, is greatly in excess of the costs in other countries. The United States has 25 percent more health care administrators than the United Kingdom, 165 percent more than the Netherlands, and 215 percent more than Germany. To put the number of administrative staff in perspective, note that on a per capita basis, the number of clinical staff is no greater in the United States than elsewhere. The United States has 10 percent more physicians per capita than Canada but 25 percent fewer physicians than the typical high-income country. Similarly, the United States has only 8 percent more nurses per capita than the typical rich country.

These administrative costs add up. Administrative cost differences account for 39 percent of the difference in spending between the United States and Canada. A good share of this might be eliminated in a single-payer system—though there are also other ways of streamlining these costs.

Additional care received is the third reason for higher spending in the United States. For any given condition, Americans are treated with more intensive care than people in Canada or most other high-income countries. A heart attack victim in the United States is more likely to receive a surgical intervention than is a similar patient in Canada; treatment of mental illness occurs more frequently (even given diagnostic symptoms); imaging is much more readily performed in the United States.[7]

There is no mystery behind this. The United States does more than other countries because it has the resources available to do so. In Ontario, there are eleven hospitals that are authorized to perform open-heart surgery.[8] Pennsylvania has approximately the same population as Ontario, but it has sixty hospitals capable of performing open-heart surgery.[9] There is simply no way that Canadian hospitals could perform open-heart surgery on as many patients as American hospitals do, even were they to operate round-the-clock. Indeed, the rate of stent insertion in Canada is half that in the United States.[10]

The differences in availability of technology across countries are startling. Considering just inpatient institutions, the United States has the fifth-highest number of CT scanners per capita (behind Japan and Australia), the second-highest number of MRI scanners per capita (behind Japan), and the second-highest number of PET scanners (also behind Japan).[11] Counting outpatient institutions would move the United States up even higher. The United States is the second-highest in stent insertions per capita (behind Germany) and the third highest in bypass surgery per capita (behind Belgium and Germany).

A single-payer system would reduce spending on treatments, provided the availability of technology was reduced. Cutting out existing treatments is hard, however. Whenever countries close down hospitals or reduce facilities, the population becomes upset, and support for the system falls.[12] It is far more effective to limit the diffusion of new technologies over time. It is much easier to tell hospitals in Ontario without open-heart surgery capabilities that such a program is not needed than to tell hospitals that already have these capabilities to close their existing programs. Thus technology restrictions have increasing bite over time.

The immediate fear about limiting the availability of technology is, of course, that necessary services will not be provided. After all, there is no guarantee that physicians and hospitals operating under technological constraints will eliminate only unnecessary surgeries or images. In some countries, the rationing works well. For example, outcomes after a heart attack are similar in the United States and Canada, even though Americans receive much more intensive treatment; there is enough gray-area care where advanced technology need not be applied that physicians in Canada do not have to cut into valuable care. Indeed, patients in Canada are not even told they are being rationed; there is simply different medical criteria for when open-heart surgery is justified and when it is not. (Lest Americans complain, rates of bypass surgery differ enormously across the United States, and there are few complaints about rationing in low-use areas.)

If rationing is not the fear, what is? There are three concerns about moving to a single-payer system into the United States. First, Americans are wary about government involvement in medical care, and a single-payer system involves more government than many people are comfortable with. There is an apocryphal story about a senator who was approached by one of his elderly constituents and told to "keep the government out of my Medicare" (oops, Medicare is a government program). Even the Affordable Care Act's individual mandate to buy private health insurance struck some people as too much government involvement in health care. Single-payer health care goes a layer deeper.

More substantively, single-payer systems are not necessarily good at encouraging people to receive good preventive care. As noted previously, the United States is relatively bad at prevention: rates of chronic disease treatment are low, and the system is not good at working with people to schedule their cancer screenings or renew their medications. It turns out that other countries are similarly bad at this. As figure 10 shows, only 46 percent of diabetics in the typical developed country receive their recommended screening. The countries that do better are the ones that deal with people in many different settings—on the phone, late at night, and so on. Countries with more traditional office visits have low rates of appropriate chronic care. Just moving to a single-payer system does not make chronic disease care work well; bigger changes in the structure of health care delivery are needed.

Finally, single-payer systems do not necessarily guarantee equal access to all citizens. Doctors ration fairly in Canada, but they do not do equally well in all countries. In Italy, for example, the northern part of the country is more politically powerful than the southern part, and hence, medical resources are greater in the north than in the south.[13] In England, the wages for nurses are not adequately adjusted for local price differences, so there is a chronic nursing shortage in London but adequate supply elsewhere.[14] Rationing without taking account of demand is always problematic.

• • •

The free marketeers take off from this last point and run with it. In the marketeer version of the world, governments are inher-

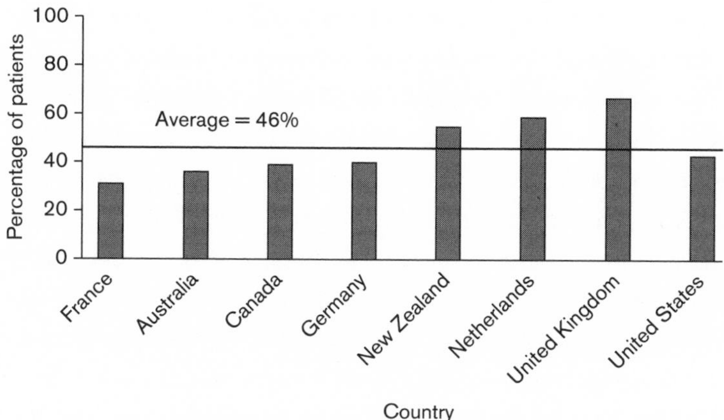

Figure 10. Share of diabetics who received recommended preventive care services, 2008. The United States is about average in the share of diabetics who received recommended preventive care services, including HbA1c screening, lipid testing, and retinal exams. Rates of diabetes control are much lower. Data are from Cathy Schoen et al., "In Chronic Condition: Experiences of Patients with Complex Health Care Needs, in Eight Countries," *Health Affairs* 28, no. 1 (2009): w1–w16, http://content.healthaffairs.org/content/28/1/w1.abstract?keytype = ref&siteid = healthaff&ijkey = cOSQSi1j6fDlo.

ently inefficient, and markets are inherently wonderful. Thus, the way to solve problems in medical care is to rely on the power of the market. That means empowering consumers and disabling governments. In the marketeer conception, health care is no different from selling toothpaste or cars; putting consumers in charge will yield the best possible outcome. Naturally, with this point of view, the marketeers tend to be right of center. Their members populate organizations such as the Cato Institute, the Heritage Foundation, and the American Enterprise Institute.

Marketeers come in two flavors: those who prefer a market with very little insurance and consumers left mostly on their own, and those who put faith in the power of private insurers to steer people to the right outcomes. Let's call the first group direct marketeers and the second insurance marketeers.

The canonical medical treatment in the direct-marketeer framework is Lasik surgery—the surgery that corrects vision problems in people who are nearsighted or farsighted, or who suffer from astigmatism.[15] There is relatively little insurance for Lasik; mostly, people pay for the surgery out of pocket. Over time, the price of Lasik has fallen, even as quality has improved. Wouldn't that be true of all medical care if consumers were in charge?

According to Newt Gingrich, it would be:

> The lesson of nearly four hundred years of entrepreneurial, technology and science-based free market capitalism is very clear. You should expect to get more choices of higher quality at falling prices. This is the opposite of the rationing mentality of some left-wing politicians and the scarcity mentality of too many bureaucrats. We need to bring these concepts into health and health care. We must insist that doctors, hospitals, medical technologies, and drugs have both quality and cost information available on-line so people can make informed decisions. We can then shift the purchasing decision to the patient and his family so they can make their own cost and quality trade-off decisions.[16]

Of course, a moment's reflection reveals the difference between Lasik and open-heart surgery. One is performed after much thought and time for shopping; the other is not. One is readily amenable to measuring quality; the other requires more analysis. One is a simple procedure; the other is complex. Move away from Lasik, and the world suddenly becomes less clear. Dental care is not well covered by insurance, and the environment is leading to healthier teeth, yet the costs of dental care have increased nearly as rapidly as the costs of medical care.[17] Even veterinary costs are increasing over time, at roughly the rate of human care, and very few people have insurance for their pets.[18]

The tenuous extrapolation from Lasik to open-heart surgery annoys many analysts. Arnold Relman, former editor of the prestigious *New England Journal of Medicine,* wrote, "A real solution to our [health care] crisis will not be found until the public, the medical profession, and the government reject the prevailing delusion that health care is best left to market forces.... Once it is acknowledged that the market is inherently unable to deliver the kind of health care system we need, we can begin to develop the 'non-market' arrangements for the system we want."[19]

The idea that markets may not be perfect does that mean that people do not respond to prices in medical care. They do. The RAND Health Insurance Experiment, conducted in the 1970s, showed conclusively that high cost sharing—either through deductibles or coinsurance rates—discourages utilization.[20] A plethora of studies since then have confirmed the RAND results. Rather, the problem is that people do not respond in the right way.

Consider the following study, a typical one in the literature.[21] Researchers analyzed the medical spending and claims information for 36,000 people in insurance plans with high cost sharing, and matched them by health status to over 700,000 people with more traditional insurance plans (to correct for differences in health between the two groups). They then examined how utilization differed between the two groups, attributing the difference (adjusted for health and demographic status) to the insurance plan. People in higher cost-sharing plans used fewer services overall. All told, the high cost-sharing plan saved 4–15 percent relative to the traditional plan. This is a modest effect; it is not huge (recall that the total amount of excess spending is believed to be one-third), but it is not trivial either. Putting everyone with insurance in a high cost-sharing plan would reduce overall medical spending by about 10 percent.

Unfortunately, the services people deferred were not always the unnecessary ones. Children in the high-deductible plans were less likely to be immunized; age-appropriate women were less likely to be screened for breast and cervical cancer; and both men and women were less likely to be tested for colorectal cancer. In the short run, deferring these services does not affect health much; missing a single screening is rarely fatal. But over time, this would worsen health and offset some of the initial health savings. Breast and cervical cancer are more expensive when detected later, and more likely to be fatal. Deferred immunizations make infectious disease outbreaks more likely. There are good ways to save money, but this is not one of them.

This study is not an isolated one; the result that cost sharing leads to modest savings, split between necessary and unnecessary care, has been found in a variety of settings.[22] One research report even estimated that higher cost sharing resulted in higher overall spending in the short run, as more people stayed off of their medications and wound up being admitted to a hospital.[23] More often, the studies show that plans with higher cost sharing save money, but not in ways that we would prefer.

On one level, this is irrational. Why should someone not get a mammogram just because the cost of the scan has increased modestly? (In some cases, the scan is even free, but the physician visit to schedule it is not.) Isn't the possibility of future breast cancer enough to get people to go in for tests? But who said people were rational? Study after study shows that charging people more for screening or for chronic care medications leads to fewer recommended screens and reduced use of those medications.[24] Wishing that people become better able to navigate health care when they pay more for it will not make these decisions different.

The insurance marketeers have a solution for this. Recognizing that people are not good at making medical care decisions on their own, they posit that insurers can help them. A good insurance company could figure out what services are valuable and what services are not. If people would benefit from outreach to schedule their screening or take their medications, then the insurance company could set up programs to do this. On the other side of the ledger, if stent insertion is not needed for people with stable coronary disease, the insurance company would not cover that use of the technology. That, after all, is the magic of the market.

I have more sympathy for this view than for the direct marketeer view. Insurers are responsive to what their customers want—more or less. The idea that insurers can help people make sense of the medical care system is not crazy.

But so far, the evidence that insurers will be effective in this task is missing. In the mid-1990s, insurers tried to steer people away from some providers and toward others. The primary care physician was going to be a "gatekeeper" who would "manage" members' care. They would do this by finding high-quality, low-cost providers and increasing use of those doctors and hospitals. Health maintenance organizations (HMOs) became all the rage.

The problem was that it didn't work as intended. In most HMOs, physicians were dictated to, rather than involved in the care planning process. Physicians do not like their professional judgment being questioned any more than the rest of us do. Patients did not understand the rationale for the restrictions, and they rebelled. Even Congress joined the act, with repeated bills proposing a Patient's Bill of Rights (none of them ever passed). By the late 1990s, people were sick enough of managed care that managed care restrictions were loosened, and the worst of the era was undone.

Reading the proposals of the insurance marketeers, one would never know that we had lived through this history. Here is 2012 Republican presidential nominee Mitt Romney: "With insurers competing against each other to provide the best value to customers, efficiency and quality will improve and costs will decline."[25] The word *HMO* barely passes his lips. Here is the House Republican Party arguing for another marketeer favorite—turning Medicare over to private companies: "A defined contribution system [as it is termed] is likely to result in lower rates of health care spending growth, since insurers would be competing on price as well as benefit design, and would be directly accountable to patient demand for high-value, high-quality services."[26] I wish the evidence supported this.

There is a clear test of the insurance marketeer theory: Medicare is largely a public system, and employer-based insurance is largely private. Thus, if the insurance marketeers' theory is correct, the cost of Medicare should be rising more rapidly than the cost of private insurance. It is difficult to test this exact prediction, since longtime series data on insurance premiums are hard to obtain, and they need to be adjusted for changes in who is covered. But a related theory can be tested. If the insurance marketeer theory is right, Medicare costs per beneficiary should be increasing more rapidly than total national medical spending per person—which reflects the average of public and private insurance.

Figure 11 shows this comparison. The prediction is wrong. Aside from a few particular years, Medicare and total spending

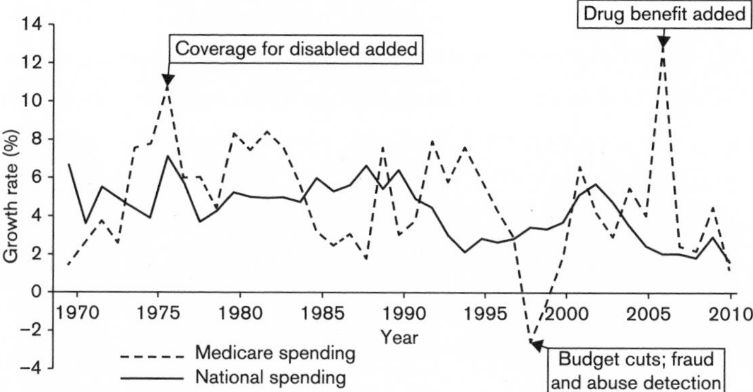

Figure 11. Growth rate of Medicare and total medical spending, 1970–2010. Data from Center for Medicare and Medicaid Services, *National Health Expenditure Accounts*, www.cms.gov/Research-Statistics-Data-and-Systems/Statistics-Trends-and-Reports/National-HealthExpendData/Downloads/tables.pdf.

have grown at about the same rate. Medicare grew faster in 1973, when it added coverage for people with kidney failure and disabilities. In 1997, Medicare enacted payment reductions and went after hospitals that were overbilling the government; the result was a dramatic decline in spending. In 2006, drug benefits were added to the Medicare program; spending growth spiked in that year. On average, growth in the two programs has been about the same. One can always believe that the future will be different than the past, but it is best not to bet the house on it.

• • •

The point that single-payer advocates and marketeers both miss is that medical care is an extremely complex business, and the operation of the business itself needs to change. Consumers are not informed enough to make real shopping work, and insurers have not stepped in to substitute for them. Indeed, the relationship between private insurers and providers is so acrimonious that it is implausible to think that private insurers will bring much standardization to medical care. Single-payer systems, while having the virtue of predictable savings, do not provide the incentives to always get care right. Thus a different model is needed. Indeed, as medicine increases in complexity, the problem with the current system will only get worse.

In fact, there is an answer to the question about where the best medical care is provided. It is not in a foreign country or a single geographic location. Rather, the answers are scattered about the United States, in organizations that have set their sights on providing the best medical care at the lowest price. There are many such organizations in operation. I take a tour of a few of them next.

CHAPTER FOUR

The Quality Cure

Amid the depressing stories about the cost and quality of U.S. health care, there are some distinct outliers. A number of health care organizations across the country have made tangible strides toward higher-quality, lower-cost performance. In this chapter, I describe some of these successes and analyze what we can learn from them about the strategies that lead to good outcomes (see table 6).

• • •

Let's start off with primary care, which is the backbone of any health system. To see primary care done well, we head to California and Kaiser Permanente. Kaiser Permanente is one of the largest health systems in the world. The plan has nine million members based largely in California and the Pacific Northwest, but its reach extends to Colorado, the District of Columbia, Hawaii, Ohio, and Georgia. Kaiser always had the reputation of monitoring hospital use carefully, but its primary care lagged. Keeping costs low too often meant having too few primary care

TABLE 6

Examples of the quality cure

Provider	Type of Care	Specific Problem	Intervention	Annual Cost Savings	Projected National Savings
Kaiser	Primary	Wasted primary care visits	My Health Manager	$500 million	$6.6 billion
Mayo Clinic	Primary	Specialist consultations	Curbside Clinics	n/a	n/a
Geisinger	Acute	Coronary artery bypass graft surgery	ProvenCare℠ Program	5% of hospital costs	$400 million
Intermountain	Acute	Elective inductions <39 weeks	Women and Newborn Clinical Integration Program	$50 million	$3.5 billion
Virginia Mason	Acute	Back surgery	Back Pain Collaborative	$1.7 million	$45 billion

physicians. In the 1990s and early 2000s, people were leaving the plan because they found Kaiser too big and impersonal.

Kaiser responded by installing the largest private electronic health system in the world. Built over six years at a cost of $4 billion, the EMR was finished in 2010. HealthConnect, as it is called, is now present in 454 medical offices and 36 hospitals.[1] The system permits patients to do many things online, ranging from requesting refills and scheduling appointments at the low end to viewing test results, sending secure e-mail to physicians, and accessing complete medical records at the high end.[2] Behind the scenes there is decision-support software that helps providers do what is best, as well as a host of analytic capabilities to analyze how Kaiser and each of its clinicians are doing.

Kaiser's system has received a huge positive response from patients, with over 58,000 registering to become part of the online community every month. The ability to connect electronically has made a major impact on the way Kaiser provides primary care.[3] In 2011, there were 105 million visits to the Kaiser website. Thirty million people viewed lab test results online, 12 million e-mails were sent to doctors and other care providers, and 10 million prescriptions were refilled online. This use of technology dramatically reduced the need for face-to-face interactions. As a result, office visits have decreased as much as 26 percent; telephone and e-mail consultation increased by eight and six times, respectively.[4]

Kaiser's e-mail system has also produced tangible health improvements. A 2010 study found that e-mail interactions led to significant improvement on a variety of quality measures, such as HbA1c testing for diabetics, LDL screening for people with high cholesterol, and blood pressure control. Kaiser is now at or near the top of national rankings in chronic disease care.[5]

The EMR system's impact on costs is difficult to measure, because nobody was laid off. Rather, the resources saved were largely freed up to serve more patients. But there were material changes. Because of the electronic record, most of an office that was in charge of handling paper records was reassigned to other tasks.[6] The consulting firm McKinsey estimated that the disease registries alone would save $3 million annually by reducing acute events.[7] Kaiser itself estimated that it would save $500 million per year thanks to its streamlined system.[8] Expanded nationally, just these savings would amount to $6.6 billion of reduced spending per year.[9] On the competitive front, patients' perceptions of Kaiser have improved markedly. Kaiser considers the computer system a competitive advantage in encouraging members to join and stay with its plan.

Of course, electronic capability isn't everything. Kaiser's payment model complements its IT system. Physicians receive a salary; thus they can substitute e-mail communication for face-to-face visits as appropriate. In addition, physicians are rewarded for measures such as workload, group contribution, patient satisfaction, and quality, through a bonus that is up to 5 percent of their salary.[10] Outside of Kaiser, in contrast, e-mail is a money loser: there is no payment for e-mail communication, and e-mail exchanges reduce the time for seeing patients face to face, which is reimbursed. The typical primary care doctor would struggle mightily to replicate the primary care system at Kaiser.

The Mayo Clinic is another example of improved primary care.[11] The Mayo Clinic is the world's oldest and largest multispecialty group practice. Founded in the 1920s, the Mayo Clinic is based in Rochester, Minnesota, and has expanded to Jacksonville, Florida, and Glendale, Arizona, in recent years. The Mayo

Clinic is known for excellent medical care, advanced medical training, and cutting-edge research.

Early on, the Mayo Clinic adopted the idea that physicians need to practice as a team, not a collection of individuals. As early as 1910, William J. Mayo (the founder of the clinic) wrote, "The sum total of medical knowledge is now so great and wide-spreading that it would be futile for any one man … to assume that he has even a working knowledge of any part of the whole.… It has become necessary to develop medicine as a cooperative science; the clinician, the specialist, and the laboratory workers uniting for the good of the patient, each assisting in elucidation of the problem at hand, and each dependent upon the other for support."[12]

Teamwork is central to the Mayo Clinic model. A patient at the Mayo Clinic has a "coordinating physician," not a primary-care gatekeeper. The physician coordinator can reach specialists immediately for quick advice; a walk down the hall often substitutes for a future appointment. Visits are scheduled with all relevant specialists in sequence, and information flow is maintained through continuously updated electronic medical records. As at Kaiser, physicians at the Mayo Clinic are paid for good care, not more visits. The teamwork model is one reason why the Mayo Clinic is nationally recognized as a quality leader in both primary and acute care.[13]

• • •

If the goal of primary care is to provide people with access in as many ways as possible, the goal of acute care is to help people when they get very sick—to do what is needed when it is needed, avoiding too much or too little. The best health systems have taken exactly this approach. They give people the right care all the time—no less and no more. To see how they do this, let's start in central Pennsylvania. Geisinger Health System is an integrated health provider serving a base of approximately 2.6 million patients throughout Pennsylvania. It is renowned for its focus on acute care, through programs such as ProvenCare^{SM}, a step-by-step process that seeks to improve quality.

Consider the example of coronary artery bypass graft (CABG, pronounced like the vegetable).[14] CABG is a surgery performed on patients with severe heart disease who have had or are at risk of having a heart attack. The procedure provides additional blood flow to the heart by transplanting or "grafting" arteries or veins from another part of the body to the heart. CABG is a difficult operation, with high operative mortality and a premium placed on the right care at the right time.

In 2005, Geisinger decided to standardize CABG care in an effort to improve quality and lower costs. It started by creating a list of best practices in CABG. Physicians at Geisinger identified forty such best practices, based on 2004 guidelines from the American College of Cardiology and the American Heart Association (figure 12). The list of best practice guidelines included five different areas in the patient's timeline of care: preadmission, during an operation, postoperative, discharge, and postdischarge. Each of the five categories includes up to twelve specific process measures, such as screening for the risk of stroke and administration of postoperative aspirin, beta-blockers, and antibiotics. Importantly, these best practices are based on clinical criteria about what is best for patients, not economic criteria about costs. At Geisinger, as at other institutions striving for more efficient care, physicians are never put in a position of denying care for economic reasons.

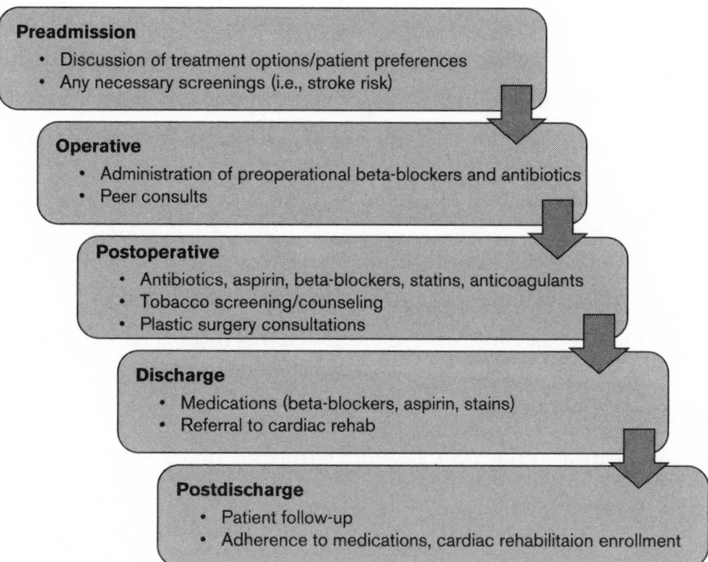

Figure 12. ProvenCare[SM] best care practice categories and examples. Forty process steps were identified, disseminated, and built into the electronic workflow.

In analyzing its CABG performance, Geisinger discovered that it was good but not great. Geisinger had low mortality and good morbidity outcomes, but it was implementing best practice in only a little over 50 percent of cases. Clearly, there was room to improve.

The workflow to achieve these goals was programmed into the electronic medical record (Geisinger has had one since 1995). When performing CABG, the right care is automatically prompted, so that the default path for physicians is the one associated with the highest quality. Doctors who choose not to comply with specific prompts must document their reasons for not doing so, and their compensation is tied to adherence (though compensation is not tied to specific patient outcomes for fear that it might provide a disincentive to take on sicker patients).

Geisinger also sought to get patients more involved in their own care through the "Patient Compact," an agreement between Geisinger and the patient to work together with the goal of improving the quality of care. By signing the contract, the patient makes eight commitments in the four areas of teamwork, family involvement, adherence to important guidelines, and prevention. The promises include asking questions so as to be informed, fully disclosing relevant health information, developing plans for each stage of the process, and attending a cardiac rehabilitation program following surgery.

The emphasis on the highest possible quality and patient engagement led Geisinger to a new pricing model. Realizing that quality improvement does not pay when money is collected per service provided and that higher quality actually means fewer services, Geisinger decided to establish a bundled payment. It would take a fixed fee and guarantee ninety days of care. This amount would cover preoperative care, the procedure itself, and any follow-up care—even that resulting from complications. In essence, Geisinger invented the warranty for health care.

After some ups and downs in the first six months, the program turned out to be an immense success. Adherence to recommended processes increased to 100 percent—that is, Geisinger hit all its core targets all the time. Furthermore, Geisinger kept its performance at that level. These changes led to material benefits for patients. There were reductions in the numbers of adverse events—including mortality and complications—shorter lengths of stay and fewer hospital readmissions. The magnitude of the health gains impressed everyone.

The financial benefits were impressive as well. Hospital costs for CABG fell by 5 percent after the program. Nationally, the United States spends about $10 billion annually on CABG surgery.[15] If the Geisinger experience could be replicated nationwide, the savings in CABG alone would be about $500 million annually.

The ProvenCare℠ system was so successful that Geisinger has expanded it to other conditions: angioplasty, hip replacement, cataract surgery, erythropoietin use, bariatric (weight-loss) surgery, and perinatal care (the first seven days after birth). If the cost of all episodes of care could be reduced by 5 percent, the savings to the health system would be in the hundreds of billions of dollars.

The Geisinger story is rare but not uncommon. Intermountain Health Care provides a similar example, focusing on the problem of preterm birth. Let's return to the example of premature elective induced labor, mentioned in a previous chapter. Clinical guidelines are clear in their assertion that early elective induction (before thirty-nine weeks) is not appropriate: it is associated with higher risk of cesarean section for the mother, greater NICU use for the baby, an increased chance of cognitive defects and mortality, and higher risk for chronic diseases later in life.[16] Even so, about 14 percent of elective inductions occur before thirty-nine weeks.[17]

The Intermountain Health Care System decided to tackle this problem. Like Geisinger, Intermountain is an integrated health system, composed of twenty-three hospitals and many clinics throughout Utah and parts of Idaho.[18] Intermountain developed the Storkbytes data system to measure what was going on and help them address the problem. Intermountain's data at the beginning of the process showed that 28 percent of elective inductions were being conducted before the recommended thirty-nine weeks.

In response, Intermountain formed a Women and Newborn Clinical Integration program and made it the program's goal to address this issue. The clinicians started off by reviewing and affirming that the guidelines about avoiding early elective induction were clinically appropriate. The clinical evaluation was based on patient outcomes, not economic appropriateness; physicians were never asked to withhold care for economic reasons.

To standardize practice around best care, Intermountain worked to educate staff and patients about the risks of early elective inductions. Perhaps more importantly, the new policy was programmed into the computer system as the default treatment. The computer routinely refused physicians wishing to schedule an elective induction before thirty-nine weeks of gestation; permission was required from either the hospital's chair of obstetrics and gynecology or an attending perinatologist.

Within a year of the program's implementation, Intermountain found that preterm elective inductions dropped to below 3 percent of induced labor. In addition, the study found decreases in complications associated with pregnancy and delivery, such as postpartum anemia.[19] The savings from the program were immense. Intermountain estimated that it saved $50 million annually from this intervention. Given the magnitude of early elective induction nationally, researchers estimate that applying this decision rule across the country would reduce total medical spending by $3.5 billion annually.[20]

One more example shows the power of the quality cure. The example comes from Seattle, Washington, and concerns a seemingly minor issue—the treatment of lower back pain. As noted in chapter 2, spine surgery is rapidly becoming the poster child for overused care.[21] In addition to its financial cost, treating back pain more intensively than is needed also involves significant time off work—which is especially costly for people in their prime working years. And when people are off work, productivity suffers and other medical conditions can arise (e.g., depression).[22]

For these reasons, appropriate treatment of back pain has become a focus for employers interested in improving care. Virginia Mason Medical Center in Seattle took on the challenge of lower back pain. Virginia Mason's interest in back pain did not arise by happenstance. In the early 2000s, Virginia Mason found itself in a difficult position when employers complained about the high cost and lengthy treatment time for routine back pain.[23] Rather than pleading that nothing could be done or arguing that the system was already ideal, Virginia Mason decided to redesign the care process for the condition.

Virginia Mason started by meeting with benefit managers of several large companies, including Starbucks, Nordstrom, and Costco. Together, they came up with five quality indicators for lower back pain treatment: low cost, evidence-based care, patient satisfaction, quick and easy access, and minimal loss of work time.[24] Virginia Mason tackled these goals with a production-system approach. They set their objective as identifying and fixing problems in the back pain "production system" in advance and as they arose, rather than observing them only after the fact.[25]

Using a simple triage system developed by physicians, Virginia Mason classified new back-pain cases into those likely to respond to physical therapy alone (the vast majority of the cases) and the smaller share of patients who needed more intensive care. The first group was routed into same-day physical therapy.

The latter group was sent to orthopedists, who had more time for them without the first group of patients hogging the schedule. Thus the severe patients were seen right away.[26]

Since starting the program in 2004, the clinic has reduced treatment times, increased patient satisfaction, and reduced costs.[27] Average treatment time fell from sixty-six days to twelve days. Patient satisfaction is at 98 percent.[28] MRI use for lower back pain decreased by 23 percent, and cost per case fell by 55 percent.[29]

Savings of this magnitude are immense. The national bill for lower back pain is about $86 billion annually. Applying the Virginia Mason strategy nationally would thus save nearly $50 billion annually.

• • •

At first glance, these successes in health care seem very different—a closed shop organization growing out of California, an integrated physician group in Minnesota, and health systems in central Pennsylvania, Utah, and Washington state. Geography is certainly not a deciding factor in doing well. Is there anything that defines high-performing organizations?

Many analysts are uncertain about this, and this uncertainty leads them to answer no. In the debate over the Affordable Care Act, proponents of some parts of the bill (including me) argued that having the federal government push transformation of the health system could lead to large cost savings.[30] Other analysts thought the high-performance organizations were too unique to be imitated, arguing that such organizations are not born overnight.

But noting that these systems are unique does not mean they have nothing in common. There are several features of high-performance organizations that can be imitated and encouraged. The famous Russian novelist Leo Tolstoy started his masterwork *Anna Karenina* with the observation that "happy families are all alike; every unhappy family is unhappy in its own way." To bring Tolstoy to the modern age, we might rephrase: successful businesses are (almost) all alike; every unsuccessful business is unsuccessful in its own way.

Successful businesses come in two varieties. The first is very small, local businesses that have a core of dedicated customers and personal involvement from the owner. The boutique clothing store with just the right look for its dedicated clientele is one example. The sole-practitioner pediatrician is another. People enjoy interacting with these businesses because they have excellent customer service, the quality of the product is often observably high, and the feeling of intimacy is valuable to the overall experience.

Most medical care is not like the sole practitioner, however. Most physicians are employed in larger groups,[31] and hospitals are big, often multicenter institutions. Running a health care system is closer to managing a chain of retail stores than a boutique establishment. The problem is that health care organizations are not adept at this. They resemble a chain of clothing stores that keeps sales information on note cards and runs the employees ragged looking for the inventory in storage. At their scale, this just doesn't work.

There are principles that work for running complex businesses. Successful health care firms have figured these out. Indeed, the Institute of Medicine recently gathered together eleven people who run some of the highest-value health systems in the country and asked them what lessons they had learned. Their list is shown in table 7. They divided the essential

TABLE 7

CEO checklist for high-value care

Foundational elements	1. Governance priority (visible and determined leadership by CEO and board)
	2. Culture of continuous improvement (commitment to ongoing, real-time learning)
Infrastructure fundamentals	3. IT best practices (automated, reliable information to and from the point of care)
	4. Evidence protocols (effective, efficient, and consistent care)
	5. Resource utilization (optimized use of personnel, physical space, and other resources)
Care delivery priorities	6. Integrated care (right care, setting, providers, and teamwork)
	7. Shared decision making (patient-physician collaboration)
	8. Targeted services (tailored to resource-intensive patients)
Reliability and feedback	9. Embedded safeguards (supports and prompts to reduce injury and infection)
	10. Internal transparency (visible progress in performance, outcomes, and costs)

SOURCE: Delos Cosgrove [president and CEO, Cleveland Clinic], Michael Fisher [president and CEO, Cincinnati Children's Hospital Medical Center], Patricia Gabow [CEO, Denver Health and Hospital Authority], Gary Gottlieb [president and CEO, Partners HealthCare System], George Halvorson [chairman and CEO, Kaiser Permanente], Brent James [executive director, Intermountain Institute for Care Delivery Research], Gary Kaplan [chairman and CEO, Virginia Mason Health System], Jonathan Perlin [president, Clinical and Physician Services, HCA], Robert Petzel [undersecretary for health, Department of Veteran Affairs], Glenn Steele [president and CEO, Geisinger Health System], and John Toussaint [CEO, ThedaCare Center for Healthcare Value], *A CEO Checklist for High-Value Health Care* (Washington, DC: Institute of Medicine, 2012).

ingredients into four groups. Foundational elements include making high-value care a priority and creating a culture of continuous improvement. Infrastructure includes electronic records and the use of protocols. Care delivery priorities are the third area; integrating care across providers and between providers and patients is the heart of this component. Finally, the CEOs stressed reliability and feedback, including embedded safeguards and transparency throughout the process.

The lessons in table 7 are specific to health care, but the principles are general. Looking across all businesses in the economy, successful firms tend to have three common organizational features, shown in figure 13. First, successful firms use IT extensively. They know what goods they are selling, how much it costs to make them, and how they can manufacture them most efficiently. Wal-Mart, one of the most productive companies in the world, was a pioneer in the use of information technology in business. It introduced scanners at checkout counters, the universal product code (UPC), radio frequency identification tags (RFID) for better inventory management, and electronic data interchange (EDI) to connect buyers and sellers.[32] These innovations save time and money. With checkout scanners, for example, Wal-Mart is able to reorder inventory without assigning an employee to tally sales and make the connection.

Our good health care firms all use IT extensively. Kaiser is famous for its IT system—$4 billion is certainly a lot to spend. Both Geisinger and Intermountain Health Care stress the role of their electronic records in ensuring that the best care is provided all the time. Indeed, I once asked the guru of Intermountain Health Care's operations, Brent James, what he considered the most important factor in Intermountain's success. He credited the information infrastructure.

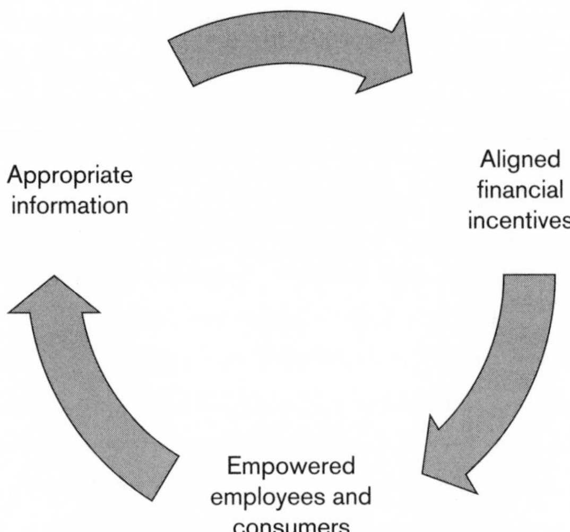

Figure 13. The drivers of productive businesses. Successful firms generally have three features in common: they use IT extensively to evaluate their practice; they align financial incentives to focus on value creation; and they engage employees and customers in quality improvement.

Second, successful firms reward doing the right thing—making products that work and having satisfied customers. Whether you agree with the Apostle Paul ("The love of money is the root of all evil") or George Bernard Shaw ("The lack of money is the root of all evil"), we cannot ignore the role of money in how the system works. In health care, this involves putting together compensation packages that reward good care and blunt external incentives for poor care. In some systems (Kaiser and the Mayo Clinic, for example), physicians are largely salaried. In other cases (e.g., Intermountain), physicians receive a performance bonus based on high quality. The compensation systems are not the same at all of these institutions, but they all have this in common: in none of the high-quality systems is a large share of physician compensation related to how intensively a doctor treats patients. Good organizations want physicians focused on the best care, not just more care.

Third, successful firms empower employees, and even customers, to make changes that improve productivity. Clearly, senior leadership needs to be supportive. But good ideas do not come exclusively, or even primarily, from the top; rather, they come from frontline workers and even customers. In many manufacturing firms, workers can stop the production process at any time if they spot a problem or need additional material; eliminating mistakes is the only goal.

In all the organizations described above, physicians and other care personnel play a key role in making the system work, by designing protocols and ensuring that they are followed or revised as necessary. This guarantees that physicians buy into the care process. Customer involvement is also key. Virginia Mason was explicitly responsive to what its customers needed from them. Similarly, Kaiser's EMR was designed with the enrollee in mind.

Information, reward structures, and decentralized decision making are what set great performers apart from good ones. Unfortunately, each of these ingredients is inadequate in health care; fixing this inadequacy is the central challenge of health care reform. In the next chapters, I show why performance in each area is poor and how we can fix it.

CHAPTER FIVE

It's What You Know

Information is vitally important in health care. When people are ill, the first thing they want from the medical system is information—what is wrong, and what can be done to fix it? Treating physicians need to coordinate information from a variety of sources—textbooks, blood tests, and images, as well as experience—to form a diagnosis. They must then refer the patient to the appropriate follow-up care, based on their knowledge of specialists and the patient's condition. Specialists must apply their own information sets to determine precise therapies and the sequencing of those therapies. All of this must be done in light of the patient's preferences and cost sharing.

Viewed as a production process (how do we produce "health restoration" given the sick patient and a variety of possible treatments?), health care is among the most information-intensive processes in the economy. And yet, the information basis on which health care makes these decisions is among the least sophisticated of any industry in the economy. Most records are not computerized, physicians are expected to keep relevant medical knowledge in their head, and details about the benefits, risks, and costs of different procedures are often maddeningly hard to track down. Consider the following scenarios:

- When you are referred by one doctor to another because of an unresolved problem, how often do you have to explain the full story again to the new doctor?
- The last time a family member received surgery, were they provided with the clinical outcome records of the doctor who operated, or was the surgeon's quality vouched for entirely by word of mouth?
- Have you or a family member ever had a test redone because the results of the first test were lost or otherwise not available at the appropriate time?

Too many people answer yes to these questions. This is symptomatic of a medical system that is unable to effectively store and access information. The result is higher cost than is necessary and lower quality than is possible. For this reason, easier and better access to information must be part of health system improvement. Put simply, no industry ever got better without knowing what it was doing.

Successful firms invest heavily in information technology. The Wal-Mart example was highlighted in the previous chapter. But Wal-Mart is not alone. American firms started investing heavily in information technology in the late 1970s and early 1980s (figure 14). This investment picked up with the Internet boom in the 1990s and has remained high. The average American firm spends about $2,700 per employee per year on computers and software. But health care is a laggard. In fact, it is one of

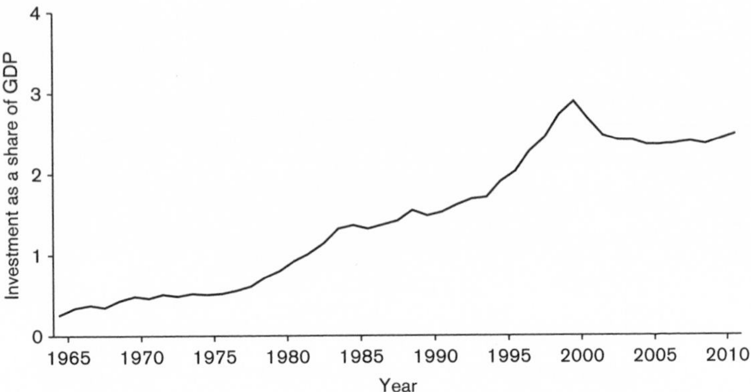

Figure 14. Nonresidential computer and software investment as a share of GDP, 1965–2011. Data for the figure are from the National Income and Product Accounts, available at www.bea.gov.

the lowest users of information technology among any industry in the economy.

• • •

There are many types of technology in health care, so let's start with some basics. IT systems are generally referred to as electronic medical records (EMRs) or electronic health records (EHRs). The two terms are mostly interchangeable; for simplicity, I use the term EMR.

An EMR is not a single set of computer code; there are layers to what a system can do. One helpful typology of systems is displayed in table 8.[1] An EMR has four functionalities. The first is storing clinical information, including patient demographics, physician notes, problem lists, and medication lists. Basic EMR systems cover much of this—all but physician notes and nursing assessments. A comprehensive EMR would cover all areas.

TABLE 8

Functions of an electronic medical record

Function	Description	Basic	Comprehensive
Electronic clinical information	Patient demographics, problem lists, medication lists, discharge summaries, advance directives	✓	✓
	Physician notes, nursing assessment		✓
Results management	Viewing lab reports, radiology reports, diagnostic test results	✓	✓
	Radiology images, diagnostic test images, and consultant reports		✓
Computerized provider order entry	Medications	✓	✓
	Lab reports, radiology tests, medications, consultation requests, nursing orders		✓
Decision support	Clinical guidelines, clinical reminders, drug allergy results, drug-drug interactions, drug-lab interactions, drug dosing support		✓

SOURCE: Dustin Charles, Michael Furukawa, and Meghan Hufstader, *ONC Data Brief: Electronic Health Record Systems and Intent to Attest to Meaningful Use among Non-Federal Acute Care Hospitals in the United States: 2008–2011*, issue brief no. 1 (Office of the National Coordinator for Health Information Technology, 2012), www.healthit.gov/media/pdf/ONC_Data_Brief_AHA_2011.pdf.

Results management is the second functionality. This involves storing reports and, in more advanced systems, images as well. In a fully electronic EMR, there is no need for radiology films (and thus no way for films to get lost). The third functionality is computerized ordering, which allows doctors to order laboratory and radiology tests, medications, and consultations electronically. Finally, decision support provides clinical guidelines and reminders, and safety checking of medication prescriptions.

To translate these functionalities into their impact on care delivery, consider the case of Betsy Lehman. Betsy was a thirty-nine-year-old mother of two. She lived in Boston and was a health columnist for the *Boston Globe.* In 1993, Betsy was diagnosed with advanced breast cancer. She chose to receive her treatment at the world-famous Dana Farber Cancer Institute in Boston, which at the time did not use electronic medical records.

Betsy enrolled in a phase one clinical trial in which she received higher than normal doses of a chemotherapy agent (cyclophosphamide).[2] Chemotherapy has certain common side effects—nausea and vomiting, for example. Too much cyclophosphamide can lead to heart failure. Betsy was supposed to receive her chemotherapy regimen on four consecutive days. The research fellow working in oncology that day calculated the dosage that Betsy was to receive given her height and weight, but he didn't know if he was supposed to indicate the total dosage or the daily dosage (the total dosage divided by four). The protocol the supervising physician had written down was unclear, and the fellow opted to write down the total dosage.

The order was sent to the pharmacy, where two pharmacists reviewed the order but did not correct or question the mistake. Nurses thought the dosage was off but did nothing about it. The net effect was that Betsy Lehman was given the cumulative clinical dosage of chemotherapy—already a high-dose regimen—on each of four days, for a total of four times the intended amount. Betsy had very bad nausea and vomiting, but more importantly, her heart was damaged. The morning she was to be discharged from the hospital, she went into cardiac arrest and died.

The error made by the Dana Farber was not discovered until months later, when researchers analyzing the data from the clinical trial Betsy was enrolled in noticed the extremely high dose of chemotherapy. It turns out that another patient fell victim to the same mistake. The other patient suffered severe heart failure, though she survived the trial (she died two and a half years later).

What caused Betsy's death? On one hand, the death was attributable to people—the physician who wrote the protocol in a confusing way, the research fellow who did not ascertain the correct dosage, the pharmacists who did not question the instructions, and the nurses who saw but did not speak. Many of them were punished. The research fellow had his Massachusetts license suspended for three years; the clinical privileges of two physicians were suspended; three pharmacists and sixteen nurses were formally reprimanded.

But more generally, the system failed. There was no standardization about how to record clinical trials, no technological way to check that medication administration was correct, and no system in place by which individuals who believed something was wrong could stop the process until they were sure it was right.

The realization that the Dana Farber had killed a patient through medical error hit the hospital like a bomb. Within two years, the president of the hospital, the chief of medicine, and many department heads had left. Fortunately for future patients, the Dana Farber took this stunning loss and used it as motivation to entirely change the information system.

Within a short time after the accidental death, the Dana Farber installed an electronic medical record with computerized provider order entry and decision support. Today, no medication is administered without the order going through the computer system. Pharmacists are not allowed to fill a prescription that is not approved by the computer review unless they have seen a study or clinical trial protocol that justifies the dosage. And the nursing staff double- and triple-check the medication dosage and identity of the patient. The Dana Farber is now among the safest hospitals around. But it took a tragedy to make it that way.

Sadly, the Betsy Lehman case is just the tip of the iceberg. Other errors have been caused by mistakes in reading handwriting, as happened in Texas in 1999 when a pharmacist misread a physician's handwriting and gave a patient a calcium-channel blocker instead of a drug to treat chest pain. The patient died.[3] It is estimated that there are 7.1 million adverse drug events each year and that universal adoption of computerized entry systems would reduce this error rate by nearly 90 percent.[4] In 2000, six years after Betsy Lehman's death, the Institute of Medicine estimated that between 44,000 and 98,000 people die annually because of errors made by the medical system.[5]

• • •

After the widely publicized death of Betsy Lehman and the Institute of Medicine study, one might imagine that hospitals and doctors' offices would rush to acquire electronic medical record systems. Sadly, this did not happen.

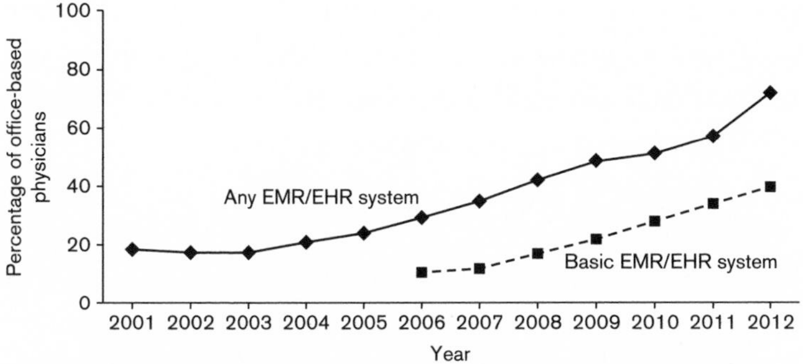

Figure 15. Adoption of EMR/EHR systems by office-based physicians, 2001–2012. Any EMR/HER system refers to a yes response to the question "Does this practice use electronic medical records or electronic health records (not including billing records)?" The basic system is as described in table 8. For description of the data and results, see Chun-Hu Hsiao and Esther Hing, *Use and Characteristics of Electronic Health Record Systems among Office-based Physician Practices: United States, 2001–2012*, NCHS data brief no. 111 (2012), www.cdc.gov/nchs/data/databriefs/db111.pdf.

Figure 15 shows the share of office-based physicians with any electronic medical record (EMR) system compared to those with at least a basic EMR system, as defined in table 8.[6] Let's focus on 2000–2009, for reasons that will become apparent. In the years 2000–2005, only 20 percent of physicians had an EMR system. As late as 2008, 42 percent of physicians had some electronic capabilities, but only 17 percent had the basic set of functionalities noted above. As a result, researchers had no doubt that Betsy Lehman-type errors were still common.

Similarly, only a small number of hospitals had invested in extensive IT systems through most of the first decade of the twenty-first century. As figure 16 shows, only 9 percent of hospitals had a basic EMR system in 2008. Per employee, hospital spending on IT was only $1,900—30 percent below the average for American industry.[7] This is more than a decade after Betsy Lehman died and eight years after the Institute of Medicine noted the ubiquity of medical errors.

• • •

Physicians and hospital executives do not deny the value of EMR systems. There has been no serious argument that the Institute of Medicine's numbers on preventable deaths are meaningfully off. Still, health care providers continually underinvest in IT. Why? Cost is the major reason cited by providers. A complete electronic medical record system costs about $20 million and about $3 million in annual operating costs.[8] Most hospitals say they do not have the money for that. Indeed, the typical hospital's annual capital budget is about $10 million.[9] How is a hospital supposed to afford an EMR?

The cost objection is important, but let's dig a little deeper. Many technologies have costs, yet they are still purchased. Over 1,600 hospitals (roughly one-third of the total) have purchased robotic surgery devices (like the da Vinci robot), at a sticker price of $1 to $2.25 million, an annual maintenance cost of $140,000, and a supply cost of nearly $2,000 per surgery.[10] Nearly 2,000 hospitals have a 64-slice CT scanner (a bit over $1 million), and nearly 900 hospitals have a PET scanner ($2.5 million and up). A number of hospitals are now investing in proton beam therapy for cancer, a $200 million technology with unproven returns in its biggest market (treating prostate cancer). What makes EMR systems different from these other technologies?

The surprising and unfortunate economics of health care is that quality improvement of the kind delivered by the EMR does not pay. Unlike new diagnostic technologies or new forms of treatment, information technology is a money loser.

To understand why this is true, consider the economics of hospital investment in a new technology—informational, diagnostic, or therapeutic. A new medical technology can affect the bottom line in three ways: it can lead to more business for the provider; it can allow the provider to charge a higher price for treating patients; or it can lower the cost of treatment. Sadly, all three disadvantage information technology investments, especially relative to their diagnostic and therapeutic cousins.

First, let's examine a therapeutic investment—the da Vinci robot. The da Vinci robot is a machine with four robotic arms controlled by a surgeon's console. The robotic arms have a greater range of motion than the human hand and can make subtler movements than a human. For this reason, many surgeons prefer it even for operations that can be done laparoscopically. So far, the robot is primarily used for prostate removal surgery, although there are other uses as well (hysterectomy and cholecystectomy for example).

Patients are attracted to hospitals with da Vinci robots. Recovery time is shorter than with traditional prostate removal surgery, so most urologists recommend robotic surgery to their prostatectomy patients. Increasingly, if a hospital wants to do prostatectomy surgery—which is fairly profitable, by the way—it needs urologists, and this requires a surgical robot.

In contrast, patients are unlikely to make their hospital choice on the basis of an EMR system. Safety statistics are not routinely reported, and even fellow physicians rarely know them. Indeed, I suspect most patients do not know whether their hospital has an electronic records system before admission.

The impact on prices is also different for IT investments than diagnostic and therapeutic investments. In the case of some technologies (although not the da Vinci robot), providers that adopt a newer technology are able to charge more for it. For example, cardiologists and hospitals are paid more for heart disease that is treated with a stent than for heart disease managed without surgical intervention. Because the amount paid is generally greater than the cost of the stent, and stent insertion is relatively easy, the economics favors the more technologically intensive care. In the case of EMRs, however, payers generally do not reimburse more for providers with an EMR (though perhaps they ought to).

The cost side of the ledger is trickier. In some settings, having an EMR can reduce costs. The two errors at the Dana Farber resulted in multimillion-dollar malpractice settlements; having an IT system in place would have prevented those errors. But the greatest cost savings from an EMR system would not accrue to the institution making the investment. Recall Intermountain Health Care and the reduction in cesarean section rates. Installing an electronic medical record and using it to monitor appropriate induction of labor helped Intermountain save $50 million annually. Cesarean sections are reimbursed more generously than vaginal births, however, so cutting back on cesarean sections reduced revenues to Intermountain. Insurers saved money, but Intermountain did not. The same was true at Virginia Mason when they reduced the number of MRIs and orthopedic consults for lower back pain. The loss there was so severe that Virginia Mason and the businesses that pushed it got the insurance companies to pay more for physical therapy so that Virginia Mason could at least do okay in that realm.

The net effect is that most clinical savings gained by operating hospitals more efficiently are not realized by the hospital undertaking the investments. As a result, hospitals tend to ignore efficiency. Researchers at the consulting firm McKinsey estimated that the cost reduction to a hospital from installing an IT system would offset only one-quarter to one-half of the installation price.[11] The rest had to be found elsewhere. In an era of tight constraints, this is a tough sell.

We can contrast the situation in medical care with that in other industries. If an automobile company builds a car that does not work, the customer returns the car, the manufacturer has to provide a new one for free, and the company absorbs the cost of shipping, administration, and the like. On top of this, the upset consumer will discourage his friends from buying there. In the case of health care, however, the economics operate backwards. If a patient is given a drug to which he is allergic, requiring a longer hospital stay, the additional care to treat the infection is reimbursed—often highly. Further, it is often not obvious if the hospital did anything wrong or nature simply went in an adverse direction. Thus provider reputations are not as responsive to good and bad care. The net effect is that IT investment is significantly discriminated against in health care relative to other industries.

There is another sense in which the economics of IT investment in health care differs from IT investment in other industries: in health care, there are spillovers across firms that are largely missing elsewhere. The benefit to any provider from investing in IT depends to a great extent on what other providers do about IT. Consider a patient who is seen at her primary care physician's office, referred to a specialist for more advanced testing, and then admitted to a hospital for a surgical procedure. For optimal management of the patient, the primary care physician, specialist, and hospital all should have shareable (termed "interoperable") medical records. That way, the specialist can have the patient's history at hand, the hospital can know about medications to which the patient is allergic, and the primary care physician can track the surgery and monitor follow-up.

But medical records are not interoperable as yet, even when they are electronic. The primary care physician, hospital, and specialist are likely to have three different computer systems—if they have IT systems at all. As a result, there is little ability to use the information stored in those systems to efficiently treat the patient. Economists term this a "network externality": the benefits of one provider adopting an IT system are higher when others have adopted a compatible system. This is true of friends who wish to share video games as well as medical care providers treating patients.

In any system with network externalities, some organization has to push the industry to invest in common standards. In the case of retail trade, the pushing organization was Wal-Mart. Wal-Mart demanded that its business affiliates operate compatible computer systems or it would not work with them; essentially all complied. In other cases, the government is the organizing agency. In the 1970s, it became clear that financial firms needed a way to route money transfers electronically from one organization to another. The National Automated Clearing House Association, an organization of commercial banks, savings banks, credit unions, and savings and loan associations aided by government, did this. The result has been enormously beneficial.

• • •

By 2008, it was clear to most experts that the information structure in health care was in need of major intervention. Something had to be done, or the situation would never get better.

Beginning in 2007, I became a health care advisor to then senator Barack Obama, and later senior health care advisor to his presidential campaign. There were several of us charged with helping to formulate health policy for the new administration. In discussing strategy, we knew that we needed to address the issue of health IT. None of us thought that IT by itself was going to cure the medical care system, but it had to be a part of the solution.

Encouraged by Senator Obama, we thought bold. We proposed to have the federal government spend $50 billion to incentivize electronic medical records. The money would subsidize doctors and hospitals that wanted to go the IT route. We chose $50 billion not because it would pay for the entire cost of the electronic systems (estimates were that the United States would need to spend $150 billion to be largely wired), but because it would pay for those providers who could not afford it and bring out the dollars to which other providers had access.

Amazingly enough, Congress took the advice to invest in IT. In early 2009, as part of the American Recovery and Restoration Act (aka the stimulus bill), Congress passed legislation supporting health IT investment. That part of the law was termed the HITECH Act, short for Health Information Technology for Economic and Clinical Health. Providers receive extra payments from Medicare for using health IT systems, and eventually they will suffer losses if they do not. Estimates at the time the act was passed suggested that HITECH would spend $30 billion on health IT, though already the amount spent has exceeded expectations. The health IT program was one of the few bipartisan parts of that contentious legislation.

The HITECH Act was well designed. Rather than allocating money to buy computers, Congress specified that IT systems must be "meaningfully used." Doctors had to use the equipment to improve care, not just own it. The Office of the National Coordinator for Health Information Technology (ONCHIT), was charged with formulating the meaningful-use criteria. Dr. David Blumenthal, who worked with me to develop the proposal, was appointed head of the office.

The first round of meaningful-use criteria was released in 2010 (after much discussion over the previous year) and specified basic functionalities such as computerized provider order entry, checks for drug interactions and allergies, and clinical decision support. Subsequent rounds will move toward complete use of medical records in all activities and making records interoperable across systems.

Following passage of the HITECH Act, and especially since the promulgation of the meaningful use criteria, use of information technology has soared. Between 2010 and 2011, hospital acquisition of EMRs doubled (figure 16). Outpatient systems have increased by nearly 50 percent in the past three years (figure 15). It is likely that in the next few years, essentially all hospitals and most physicians will have adopted electronic medical record systems.[12]

• • •

Reducing errors and promoting coordination in care is one aspect of information technology, but there are others as well. Good health care requires that patients be involved in care decisions, and information technology has enormous potential to help us accomplish this.

Consider the following scenario: a sixty-two-year-old man is diagnosed with localized prostate cancer after a biennial blood test shows an elevated level of PSA (prostate-specific antigen). The diagnosis is confirmed by biopsy. The man is trying to

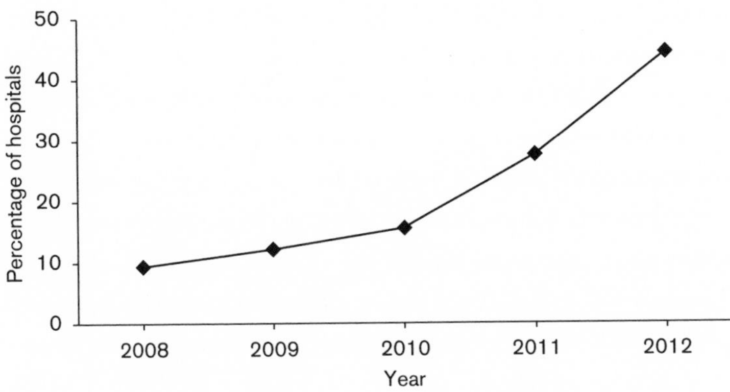

Figure 16. Adoption of basic EHR systems by hospitals, 2008–2012. Data are from Dustin Charles, Jennifer King, Vaishali Patel, and Michael Furukawa, *Adoption of Electronic Health Record Systems among U.S. Non-federal Acute Care Hospitals:* 2008–2012, ONC data brief no 9 (Washington, DC: Office of the National Coordinator for Health Information Technology, 2013), www.healthit.gov/sites/default/files/oncdatabrief9final.pdf.

decide what to do—have his prostate removed (likely using the da Vinci surgical robot noted above), undergo radiation, or wait and see if the tumor remains small. The choices have different clinical and financial implications. Prostate removal is associated with high rates of impotence and incontinence but may stem a growing tumor. Radiation is nonsurgical, but it too can cause side effects.[13] Radiation is also more expensive than surgery. Watchful waiting, known as active management, is ideal if the cancer is unlikely to progress rapidly (the vast bulk of prostate cancers do not) but would be inappropriate for a rapidly developing cancer. Active management costs less than the other options.

When men are surveyed about their preferences, they express strong views. Some men are desperate to see the cancer removed;

they have no tolerance for letting the cancer grow. Others care greatly about sexual function or bladder control, and thus may choose to wait. To make the decision about treatment, the man needs information on the clinical benefits and risks of different treatment paths and the financial cost of each procedure.

The financial consequences of various treatment options are large, given that many people have high rates of cost sharing.[14] They should be relatively easy to determine. Insurers know the price schedule for different options, depending on the procedure and who performs it, so they could tell people what they would pay for each option at each provider. Unfortunately, insurers generally do not provide this information. Most insurance information systems are not set up to evaluate prices, and they have not invested in systems that would be capable of doing so. Thus, despite the fact that the decision is important, most people are not able to factor cost into their treatment decision.

Relaying the clinical consequences of different options is generally in the hands of doctors. But here too the system works poorly. Let us start off by observing that men are eager for clinical information on the different options and their consequences; they look on the Internet for information, read clinical studies, and ask questions of their doctors. When men are offered structured decision videos showing the different treatments and the potential consequences of each, they are grateful to have this information, and they make decisions they are comfortable with.[15] But this information is rarely provided in a systematic way, and as a result it often does not factor into the decisions that men actually make, or are led to make. One study showed that men who were about to receive radiation therapy were no more likely to prefer that treatment option than men who were about to receive surgery—and vice versa.[16] Another study showed that many more men prefer watchful waiting than actually followed that treatment path;[17] instead, physicians steer people toward more aggressive treatment.[18]

Information technology can be used to address each of these shortcomings. Insurers should be required to show people the financial consequences of different decisions in real time—by telephone and over the web. Employers buying insurance should insist on this, and federal and state governments should require it for people insured through public programs. Doctors should be alert for better ways to inform patients about their care choices and consequences. Insurers can help by agreeing to pay more to providers that use decision-aid technologies. Since people are often less aggressive than their doctors, this may even save money. Patients should insist on having full information before they make such consequential decisions. It is, after all, their decision.

The best analogy to information about care decisions may be the decision to buy a car. Before the IT era, shopping for an automobile was stressful and unpleasant. Dealers had all the cards, and consumers were at their mercy. No one enjoyed the experience. Now that consumers are better informed, some of the fear of automobile shopping has diminished. I often ask audiences a simple question: which is more enjoyable, interacting with the medical care system or buying a used car? In most of my audiences, people would rather buy a used car than interact with the medical system. Indeed, there is a nervous giggle when they realize that everyone else feels the same way. That is not a good sign.

• • •

The impact of IT systems extends far beyond the doctor's office and the patient's computer. Information technology is a fundamental aspect of reducing administrative costs. Consider a classic administrative cost—the cost to physicians of submitting and obtaining reimbursement for the services they provide. To be concrete, imagine a physician who performs an MRI and sends a bill to the patient's insurer. The physician then learns that the insurer will reimburse the MRI only if it was medically necessary. The insurer might require documentation of a working diagnosis with relevant test results and prescriptions. To receive payment, the physician has to provide this documentation. Unfortunately, this information is often in the patient's paper record, so someone in the physicians' office needs to photocopy the relevant documents and mail or fax it to the insurer. The time and effort involved in these tasks are built into the doctor's operating costs and ultimately paid for through higher reimbursement rates to doctors, which are passed on in higher insurance premiums.

Electronic medical records can help reduce these costs. When the patient's record is electronic, the physician's assistant can simply print it out and send it to the insurer. This is significantly easier than the copying and faxing currently used. But technology can do even more. If the electronic medical record were integrated with the billing system, no printing, mailing, or faxing would be required. Instead, the relevant documentation could be shared automatically with the insurer, on an as-needed basis. Indeed, one can imagine the day when the insurer does not need the documentation at all. The doctor could attest that decision-support software approved the MRI, having checked beforehand for the relevant diagnosis and prescription. The insurer could use the decision-support software's approval as proof that the image was medically necessary.

Eliminating the need for people to do tasks better handled by computers is one of the hallmarks of successful businesses. Wal-

Mart was the first big business to link its computer systems so that products purchased at a store could be automatically reordered, without any need for human involvement. Information technology in health care could have the same effect.

In my work with a PhD student, Beth Wikler, and a practicing physician, Peter Basch, I have tried to estimate what such an information revolution would mean for administrative costs in health care.[19] Our estimate is that better use of information technology could save over $40 billion annually. That is over $100 per person per year. Even this is a conservative estimate, since it only scratches the surface of integrating information. Recall that total unnecessary administrative costs are as much as six times this amount. A technologically driven health care system will never match the low administrative costs of having only one payer with simple rules, but it can come close.

. . .

Nothing goes unchallenged in health care, and so it is with the value of health IT. Though the HITECH Act received general praise, it was also attacked. How do we know that health IT will really contribute to more efficient, lower medical care costs?

Though a number of studies have looked at this question, aggregate data are hard to come by. Researchers at the RAND Corporation did the most famous study of the benefits of health IT. In 2005, they estimated that near-universal adoption of health IT could save $80 billion annually.[20] Their analysis was not sophisticated; their biggest savings were from people being able to leave the hospital sooner because inpatient records were electronic. They had essentially no savings from the process or administrative changes noted above. But people focused on the article, given the precision it embodied.

Imagine the situation, then, when a study by the same group concluded in 2012 that the health IT experience was "disappointing" and the impact of health IT on efficiency and quality was "mixed."[21] Critics pounced on the study, the Obama administration's approach to health care, and the people who put it together. Was one leg of health reform failing before our eyes?

Actually, no. The authors of the later RAND study made an important distinction: "In our view, health IT's failure to quickly deliver on its promise is not due to its lack of potential but to shortcomings in the design and implementation of health IT systems."[22] As of 2012, when the assessment was made, health IT was still in the dissemination phase. The technology was nowhere near ubiquitous. Further, many systems were not—indeed, still are not—interoperable, and some benefits await that functionality. And many organizations have not complemented IT investment with appropriate workflow changes. It takes a while to learn how to use an entirely new system and reconfigure practices to benefit from it. I expect that seven years from now, the conclusion about health IT will be very different.

• • •

I have no doubt that greater use of information technology will be good for health care. But there are bound to be side effects. Perhaps the most important side effect will be the gradual elimination of the small family practitioner. Big firms can afford to spend a lot on information technology; small firms cannot. My employer, Harvard University, has a large IT department whose staff oversees the university's network, manages computer purchases and hookups, installs new software, and ensures the system is secure. My home has no similar person—unless you count me as the frustrated IT personnel when the computer doesn't work.

With incentives for providers to go electronic, and soon penalties for not going electronic, individual providers will be faced with a difficult choice. They will have to make a decision about whether to manage an IT system in addition to a clinical practice or instead to join a larger group. Many physicians will choose to join larger groups. Even small hospitals may find it difficult to compete with bigger hospitals that can afford larger IT staffs and increased levels of technical sophistication.

In this sense, health care is no different from the rest of the economy. In virtually every industry, the revolution in information technology has led to firms increasing in size. Retail trade used to be small and local; today, it is dominated by big firms like Wal-Mart and Amazon. Banking used to be local; now, it is national. Even law firms have spread nationally and internationally, in part because they can better share information for large clients that way.

We already see signs of this in health care. The share of physicians who practice in small groups decreases markedly with age (figure 17). Over 40 percent of doctors who are sixty-five or older work individually or in two-person practices, compared to less than 5 percent of doctors under thirty-five.

Further, practices are changing rapidly. Figure 18 shows that solo and two-person practices declined from 41 percent of all physicians in 1996–98 to 33 percent of physicians in 2004–5. Physicians have increasingly moved into medium-size practices of between six and fifty physicians. The need for IT resources is one reason for this shift, and it will continue to drive this trend.

The urge to merge holds at the hospital level too. Large hospital systems are much more likely to have EMRs than individual

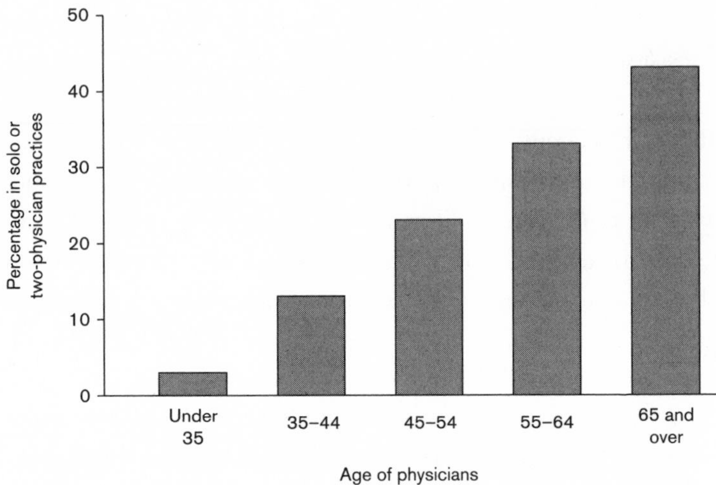

Figure 17. Share of physicians in solo or two-physician practices, by age. Data are from the Community Tracking Study for 2004–2005. Allison Liebhaber and Joy M. Grossman, *Tracking Report—Results from the Community Tracking Study: Physicians Moving to Mid-Sized, Single-Specialty Practices,* report 18 (Center for Studying Health System Change, 2007), www.hschange.com/CONTENT/941/941.pdf.

hospitals or smaller systems. In a 2011 study, for example, 43 percent of large hospitals had an EMR, compared to 21 percent of small hospitals.[23] Large hospitals also have more discretionary income than smaller hospitals. In the typical large American city, the largest hospital system garners 28 percent of the admissions and 35 percent of the profits.[24] With a large share of patients and an even greater share of profits, large systems have more resources to invest in IT, more room to undertake organizational changes, and more capacity to withstand payment reductions. This is a recipe for provider systems to get bigger.

In my home area of Boston, the expensive end of the health care market is dominated by the largest provider system, Part-

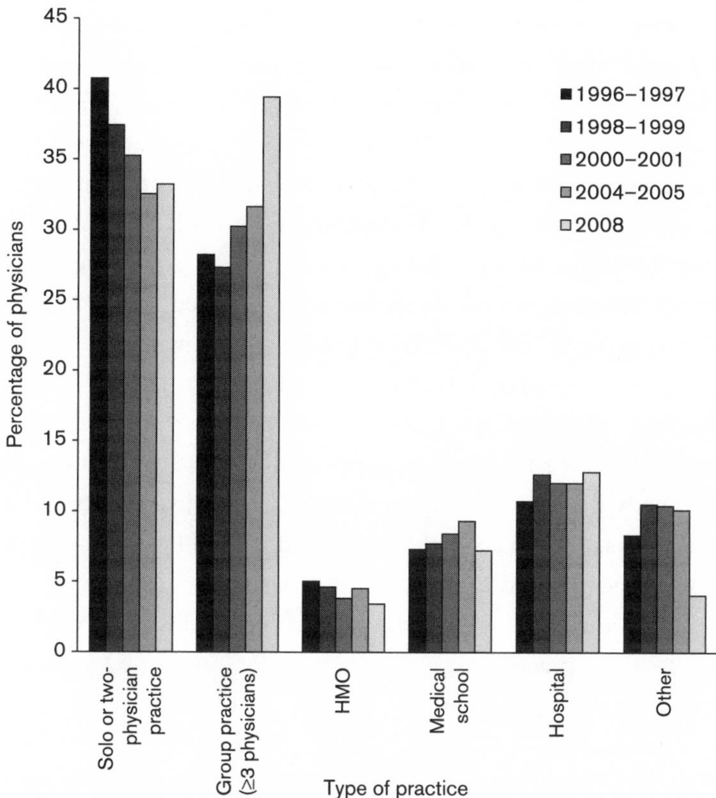

Figure 18. Variations in size of physician practices. Data are from the Community Tracking Study. Allison Liebhaber and Joy M. Grossman, *Tracking Report—Results from the Community Tracking Study: Physicians Moving to Mid-Sized, Single-Specialty Practices,* report 18 (Center for Studying Health System Change, 2007), www.hschange.com/CONTENT/941/941.pdf.

ners HealthCare—an organization anchored by Massachusetts General Hospital and the Brigham and Women's Hospital. According to the attorney general of Massachusetts, Partners' hospitals and doctors receive higher reimbursement rates than do doctors and hospitals elsewhere,[25] and Partners' financial reserves dwarf those of other institutions.[26] With the other hospitals in the market struggling to keep up, the gap between the haves and the have-nots is likely to grow. Indeed, it may be that competition for the dominant system will ultimately come not from local providers but from national systems. People in Boston will not go to Duke University Hospital for routine care but might go there for brain surgery—as the late Senator Edward Kennedy did. Or they may go to the Cleveland Clinic for heart surgery, as Lowe's recently announced it would do for many of its cardiac procedures.

Most analysts have mixed emotions about the likely decline of the small practitioner. Many mourn the loss of the tight connection between patient and provider that often accompanies the small office. Others worry that large providers will drive up prices; after all, who can afford to offer a health plan in Boston that does not allow patients to be admitted to the two most prestigious hospitals in the area? On the flip side, others believe that organizational change is only possible when providers are more integrated, and thus integration is a precursor to clinical savings.

What large firms do when they are dominant in a market depends on how they interpret their mandate. Many big firms lead the "quiet life of the monopolist."[27] They invest little in new products or processes, charge high prices, and content themselves with making a good living off of their superior position. This was part of the problem in the American automobile industry for many decades. Other dominant firms see themselves as continually threatened and live life always on edge. Wal-Mart was famous for believing it was always a price increase away from losing customers, even as it became the largest retailer in the world.

How the dominance of large medical care providers gets translated in the market depends on what the market for health care services looks like. When competition is vigorous, as it has become in retail trade, large firms take advantage of efficiencies of scale to lower prices. When profits are easy, in contrast, the quiet life is the preferred course. Thus the ultimate impact of information technology on health care will depend on how much providers need to compete for patients. And this leads directly to the issue of payment: how will doctors and hospitals get paid for what they do? I turn to this topic next.

CHAPTER SIX

Pricing the Priceless

"Follow the money," FBI agent Deep Throat was reported to have told *Washington Post* journalists Bob Woodward and Carl Bernstein as they investigated the Watergate scandal during the Nixon administration. To understand health care, there is no better advice. The way health care is reimbursed has an enormous influence on what is done, and health care reform needs to account for this.[1]

Money does not have the immediacy in health care that other considerations do. When a physician encounters a patient in pain, little else matters until the pain subsides. Instead, money is like the electricity flowing through a house: it is there, but its mechanisms are unseen. We live very differently with electricity than people did without it, yet we rarely spend much time thinking about what electricity does for us (except when the power goes out).

To see the importance of money in medical care, let's go back to the mid-1960s and the birth of Medicare. Prior to Medicare, only one-quarter of the elderly had decent health insurance.

Since the vast bulk of the elderly were relatively poor, they had little ability to pay for care out of pocket. Overall spending on care for the elderly was limited, and medical treatments were oriented toward other groups.

Medicare led to two fundamental changes. First, it was a financial godsend for the elderly.[2] The high reaches of spending used to bankrupt people. Under Medicare, it no longer did. Second, the creation of Medicare led to a fundamental change in the focus of the medical system. The number of hospital admissions, personnel, and surgical treatments for the elderly soared after Medicare. Technology blossomed, especially for older people and in areas of the country where relatively few elderly had coverage prior to Medicare. One study suggests that Medicare by itself led to a 23 percent immediate increase in hospital usage, with even larger effects down the road.[3]

Over time, this transformation of the health system led to improved health for the elderly population. Where once chronic disease was seen as untreatable and essentially fatal (René Dubos, the famous biologist and author, noted in 1969 that "modern medicine has little to offer for the prevention or treatment of chronic and degenerative diseases that dominate the pathological picture of technologic societies"),[4] over time it became amenable to medical intervention. For the first time in human history, mortality stemming from diseases of old age declined. Today, reaching age sixty-five is associated with more secure insurance coverage, greater use of medical care, and lower mortality.[5]

Of course, it is not just the availability of Medicare that affects people. The details of the policy matter too. An insurance policy that covers very few services, pays doctors poorly, and requires significant out-of-pocket payments would not be of much benefit to people. Medicare is so valuable in part because it is generous. In contrast, Medicaid payments are so low that many physicians do not accept patients with Medicaid.

But Medicare is problematic in some of its payment policies. In particular, Medicare pays on what is termed a "fee-for-service" basis, and this payment basis has been extremely detrimental. The issue of payment is complex, so let's start with an example. An elderly man has progressive blockage of the arteries supplying blood to his heart. At first, his primary care doctor and a cardiologist manage his condition. One day, he has a heart attack and is taken to the emergency department. He is diagnosed by the emergency room physician and referred to a cardiologist at the hospital, who inserts a stent to open the blocked artery. Four days later, the man is discharged with an armful of medication and a referral to a new cardiologist.

There are several ways insurers could pay for this. The traditional approach is to pay separately for each service—each visit to the primary care physician or cardiologist would be reimbursed separately, the physician who inserted the stent would bill for that service, the hospital would receive a per-day payment for the admission, and so forth. Alternatively, some of these fees could be grouped, or "bundled," together. For example, a single price might cover everything associated with the hospitalization—from the hospital days to the stent to the emergency room care. An even broader bundle would cover the entire heart attack episode, from the emergency department through months of rehabilitation. The broadest possible payment would cover all care for the person during the year; the entire physician group would then be responsible for managing the costs of the episode.

The basis of most medical care is fee-for-service reimbursement. This is the first model described: every time a patient has contact with a doctor, the doctor bills for the service provided. Hospitals do the same.

Though this system seems reasonable—fee-for-service reimbursement is used in grocery stores and retail chains—its effects can be pernicious. Go back to the man with the heart attack. One helpful step in his care and recovery is coordination. The primary care physician needs to coordinate with the various cardiologists, the cardiologists need to speak among themselves, and so forth. There is no billing code for coordination, however. A physician seeing a patient is a (reimbursable) medical event; talking to a specialist about his or her diagnosis is not. Thus visits are common, but coordination is limited. Since coordination is so necessary for solving patients' problems, this leads to tremendous inefficiency.

There is a related problem with fee-for-service payment, even when the services are reimbursed. Insurers set prices for different services, but those prices are not necessarily equal to the costs of providing that care. When payment exceeds costs, there is an incentive to do more. When reimbursement falls below cost, in contrast, doctors trying to get by will do less.

Imagine three Medicare beneficiaries who have a heart attack on the same day.[6] The first patient is rushed to the hospital and treated with clot-busting drugs but no surgery. On average, the hospital would receive about $6,000 for this patient; a variety of physicians would be paid as well. The second patient receives a stent insertion. The reimbursement to the hospital would be about $10,000, and the cardiologist inserting the stent would earn about $500. The third patient receives bypass surgery. Since this is much more intensive, reimbursement to the hospital is about $20,000, with another $2,000 or so to the cardiothoracic surgeon. These payment formulas are pretty typical;

private insurers generally match Medicare's payment structure—though they up the payment a bit. To put these amounts in perspective, Medicare pays about $38 for a typical primary care office visit.

Of course, stent insertion costs more than medical management, so it is natural to pay the cardiologist more for it. But the costs of the stent insertion are nowhere near as high as what doctors and hospitals receive for doing it. A routine stent implantation can be performed relatively quickly—about two hours of operating room time and some time for preparation and recovery. Given the high reimbursement rate, squeezing in an extra stent patient is highly lucrative. Office visits are much less so. Thus interventional cardiologists earn more than their noninterventional colleagues, and the most intensive interventionists receive the most. Cardiothoracic surgeons earn on average $525,000; cardiologists (interventional or not) earn about $400,000; and internists earn about $200,000.[7]

At the hospital level, the same is true. A large share of hospital profits comes from providing intensive services to well-insured patients—think cardiology and orthopedics. Hospitals clamor for the latest technology in these areas and fight to line up the most prestigious surgeons. Few hospitals push to be known as the "best noninterventional institution."

The result is a bias toward doing more. If the patient is at all a candidate for surgery, go ahead and operate. After all, the patient should benefit, and the reimbursement is generous. And why would a young doctor with a mountain of medical debt rationally choose to enter primary care, with its $200,000 or lower annual salary, when he or she could earn twice as much as a specialized surgeon? One can feel good doing both, but intervention is so much more lucrative.

Adding to the monetary reward of doing more is a major non-monetary "reward": reducing the probability of being sued. Physicians regularly fear that they will be sued if they do not do everything possible—and with good reason. Studies show that at least three-quarters of physicians will be sued at least once in their lifetime, and that probability rises to nearly 100 percent for some specialties.[8] Being sued does not cost physicians financially; doctors have insurance that covers payouts and legal fees. But the time and effort involved in defending a malpractice suit, along with the sense that one's professional ethics are being questioned, make physicians leery about stopping short.

The lesson is clear: *paying more for some types of care than for others creates a bias toward better-reimbursed treatment choices. It also silos medical care when coordination is needed.*

How large are these distortions? Two examples show that they can be very large indeed. First, consider Medicare payments for hospital care. From its creation in the mid-1960s up to the early 1980s, Medicare paid for inpatient stays entirely on a "fee-for-service" basis: every service that was provided had a specific price, and Medicare paid the prices that were charged. Thus extra days in the hospital brought in additional revenue, as did more tests. Even an aspirin was charged (the price was high—several dollars per pill; the profits went toward general hospital overhead).

Experts studying this system noted that hospital stays were long—too long, in fact. The experts urged Medicare to move to a "bundled" payment system. Enacted by Congress in 1983, the so-called Prospective Payment System gives hospitals a single reimbursement for each admission. The reimbursement covers all tests, equipment, supplies, and days of care that are provided (but not physician fees). The amount paid varies with the patient's

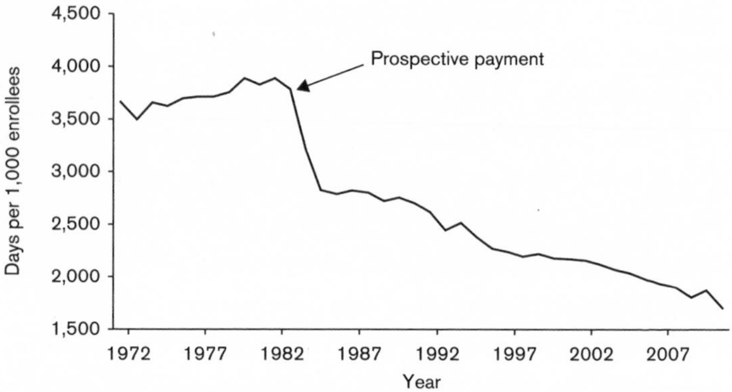

Figure 19. Medicare trends in total days of care at short-stay hospitals, 1972–2011. The cumulative decline in inpatient days is 56 percent. Data are from Centers for Medicare & Medicaid Services, *2011 Medicare and Medicaid Statistical Supplement* (Washington, DC: GPO, 2011), table 5.1, www.cms.gov/Research-Statistics-Data-and-Systems/Statistics-Trends-and-Reports/MedicareMedicaid-StatSupp/2011.html.

diagnosis and the type of surgery involved (a heart attack treated by bypass surgery is reimbursed at a higher level than one treated medically), but not with how long the patient is in the hospital or what imaging is provided during the admission.[9]

How did this payment change affect hospital care? Figure 19 provides the answer. The number of days in the hospital for Medicare beneficiaries fell by more than a quarter within three years of implementing the new system.[10] Recall that additional days went from well reimbursed to not reimbursed at all. Thus hospitals saved a bundle by reducing utilization. The change was so fast that policymakers were stunned. Who knew there was such excess?

As is the norm in health care, private insurers followed the lead of Medicare, and bundled hospital payments rapidly became the most common form of hospital reimbursement. This, in turn, led to a remarkable reduction in hospital utilization.[11] Between 1980 and 2009, the number of hospital days in the country fell by one-third, even though the population is expanding and aging. Consequently, hospitals have closed. Nationally, there were 17 percent fewer hospitals in 2010 than in 1980. Many of the survivors have merged into larger groups.

The obvious question is whether patient health suffered as hospitalizations became shorter. "Quicker and sicker" was the worry at the time. Federal officials commissioned a series of studies to examine patient health in response to the bundled payment system. The researchers examined detailed patient records from before and after the payment change to measure what happened to people and how their health was affected. At the end of the day, there was very little evidence of adverse health outcomes.[12] Patients were discharged from the hospital sooner, but by and large their health was not compromised. In essence, the reduction in hospital use was pure benefit.

Does this mean that doctors and hospitals were milking the old system to make money at the expense of taxpayers and sick elderly folks? I suspect the answer is no. It is not that physicians and hospital administrators saw a chance to make oodles and ran with it. Rather, they had an impressionistic view about the right care—a longer stay allows extra monitoring, so it must be valuable—and they never questioned that view until the money flow encouraged them to do so. When they really looked at the care process, they found that a lot of waste could be eliminated.

Consider a second example, this time from oncology. Many chemotherapy medications are delivered to oncologists' offices. For such medications, the oncologist buys the drug, and Medicare reimburses the oncologist for the medication, along with an administration fee. In the early 2000s, the amount Medicare paid oncologists for the drug was above what oncologists were paying for drugs. The reason is bulk discounts. Medicare was reimbursing physicians based on the wholesale price of the drug, but oncologists bought many drugs at a discount below wholesale. Thus Medicare was overpaying. Congress responded by lowering the reimbursement for the overpriced drugs. Since some drugs were overpriced and others were not, the reimbursement to oncologists fell for some treatments but not others.

A recent study looked at the impact of these reimbursement changes on treatment of patients with lung cancer.[13] Lung cancer makes a natural case study because there are two broad chemotherapy options—one whose price was reduced and another whose price remained constant. The authors showed that oncologists reduced use of the drugs whose prices had declined and increased use of the drugs whose prices remained constant.

Even with this change, oncologists would have lost money because of the reimbursement reduction. But here is the kicker. To offset the income reduction associated with lower procurement prices, oncologists treated more patients with chemotherapy. Even with the lower prices, chemotherapy was still reimbursed above cost. Thus income preservation entailed greater use of medication.

This finding has played out several times. Reimbursement rates for cardiac surgeons were reduced in 1980; surgeons responded by doing more surgery, where the margins were still high even after the price reduction.[14] Recognizing this behavior, officials charged with estimating the financial impact of payment changes in Medicare assume that any price reduction will reduce spending by less than the intended amount; the rest is assumed to be lost because of volume increases among physicians.[15]

The cat and mouse game between insurers and providers has many adverse effects. Pay less, get less. But if you pay too much less, doctors will offset the decrease by providing more care. It all makes sense, but it is maddening. What is a system to do?

• • •

Let's start by simplifying the problem. We will distinguish first between payment to a group of providers (the Mayo Clinic) and payment to an individual provider (a particular doctor at the clinic). I consider here the payment to the group of providers; in the next chapter, we'll come back to the individual provider.

How should a provider group be paid for the care it provides? While the current system is clearly imperfect, it is worth stressing that there is no perfect system lurking out of sight. Without knowing exactly which care should be provided and which care should not, it is difficult for any insurer to target reimbursement perfectly. For example, the ideal reimbursement for stent insertion depends on whether the stent was appropriate, in which case reimbursement should be equal to the cost of the service, or whether it was inappropriate, in which case it should not be covered. Given the many uncertainties associated with determining appropriateness and cost, insurers are not in a position to design perfect reimbursement systems.

Hence we must inherently think about a less-than-perfect situation. Economists term this a "second-best" situation; what do we do when the best possible arrangement cannot be achieved? Many factors enter into the second-best reimbursement, but the most relevant one concerns the motivation of doctors. How altruistic are doctors relative to their desire to earn more?[16] Suppose providers are like Gordon Gecko: they do whatever they can to make money, regardless of the ethics of the situation.

In this setting, payments have to be made for every valuable service, and they had better be high. Bundling payments for an episode of care will be awful, since every service provided adds to costs but not revenue, and hence will be underprovided. Conversely, suppose all doctors are like Dr. Meredith Grey of *Grey's Anatomy*: they will do whatever is needed to diagnose and treat their patients. For such physicians, bundled payments make more sense. By eliminating the financial incentives distorting care one way or the other, doctors will do just what is appropriate.

As we have seen, physicians are by and large extremely responsible in the way they administer care. When they shift around treatments, it is often in the "gray area," where it is not clear which treatment is really needed. An extra day in the hospital wasn't really that valuable; the lung cancer patients get more care, not less, when money is scarcer. So far, there are no claims in the literature that changing fees lead to substantial adverse effects on patient health. This suggests that we need not worry about major stinting of care. Rather, the key is to design a payment system that encourages coordination and the right care decisions, not just doing more to make money.

In the typology above, the conclusion is clear: *insurers should bundle all the services that are provided for a typical patient into a single amount.* When the money follows the patient as a whole—not a specific set of treatments—physicians will think about the patient as a whole and make decisions on that basis.

• • •

To draw out how bundling would work, let's take another look at a conceptualization of health presented in a previous chapter. Figure 20 shows the types of care that people receive. People

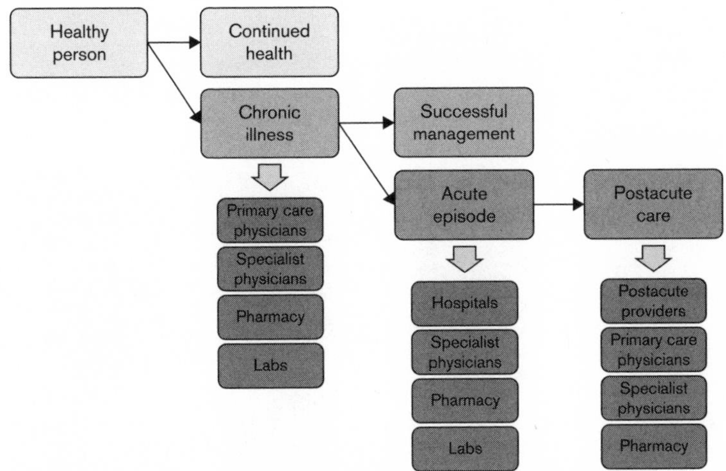

Figure 20. The organization and financing of medical care. People who are healthy use few medical services; chronic illness is associated with more service use; and acute events are associated with much more. Generally, too little is spent when people are healthy or dealing with chronic illness.

can be categorized in various stages of health—good health, with chronic disease, and having an acute episode. Associated with each health state is a set of buckets for the services that may be used: primary care, specialty care, pharmaceuticals, hospitals, and so on.

The fee-for-service system reimburses each bucket separately. A bundled payment system groups some of these buckets together. In practice, there are several ways this can be done. The easiest for most specialist physicians to adjust to is paying for an episode of care. Consider again the man who shows up in the emergency department with a heart attack. He needs acute care (medications, perhaps surgery, monitoring, etc.) and postacute care (cardiac rehabilitation, additional medications, and further

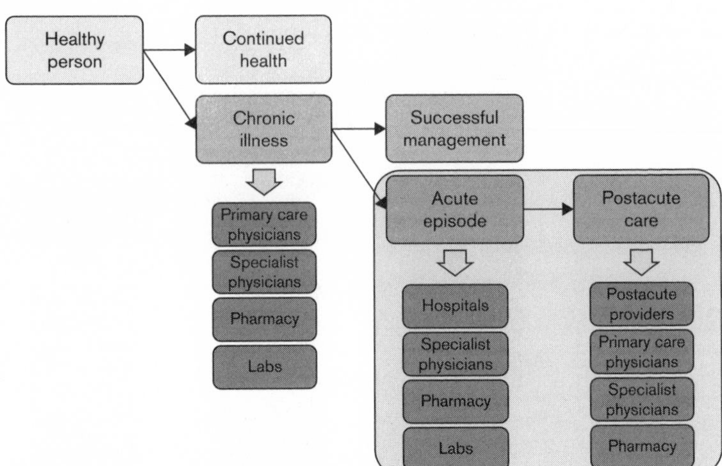

Figure 21. Bundling payment by episode. A system of bundled episode payments would group together the services provided in acute and postacute care situations.

testing). A bundled payment system would pool all care received within some period of time—for example, 180 days from the heart attack—into a single payment (figure 21). The group of providers accepting the payment would then divvy up the money among the various individuals involved—the hospital, the specialist, providers of postacute care, surgeons, and so on—as they see fit. Generally, they will do this by a prespecified agreement rather than on a case-by-case basis. For example, a hospital might have a relationship with one or more cardiac rehabilitation programs to ensure adequate follow-up care and timely communication. The hospital might pay the rehabilitation program a per-case fee to provide these services for patients in need.

There are several advantages to such a payment system. One major benefit is that most physicians are quite familiar with it. Specialists understand the idea that people need care during an episode of illness, and they like to follow patients throughout this experience. If cardiologists are asked whether they can conceptualize managing acute and postacute care for a person with a heart attack, they will readily answer that they can. The same is true for orthopedists treating musculoskeletal problems and oncologists treating cancer. Further, a large share of spending occurs in acute and postacute settings, so that bundling care at this level provides a potential for major savings.

However, one difficulty with this system is that of determining which services are included in an episode and which are not. If a patient who had a heart attack goes back to his or her physician for a routine check-in, is it related to the cardiac disease or not? It is difficult to attribute a single cause to all services. A second drawback of this system is that it does not incentivize prevention of the acute episode in the first place. If only acute care is bundled, providers gain nothing by preventing the heart attack.

This latter concern has led to a second type of payment system, which would reward primary care physicians for successful prevention of acute disease. Such a system is shown in figure 22. Helping healthy patients maintain their health or assisting patients with chronic disease to manage their health would be rewarded; groups of physicians that were not as good at preventing disease progression, in contrast, would earn less. The measure of outcomes is key here. Many such measures might be designed—for example, heart attacks that actually occur relative to those that occurred in the past, or avoidance of emergency care for nonacute conditions. Because a payment system based on primary care management works on a different margin from the bundled episode payment (largely primary care versus largely specialty care), they are often proposed together.

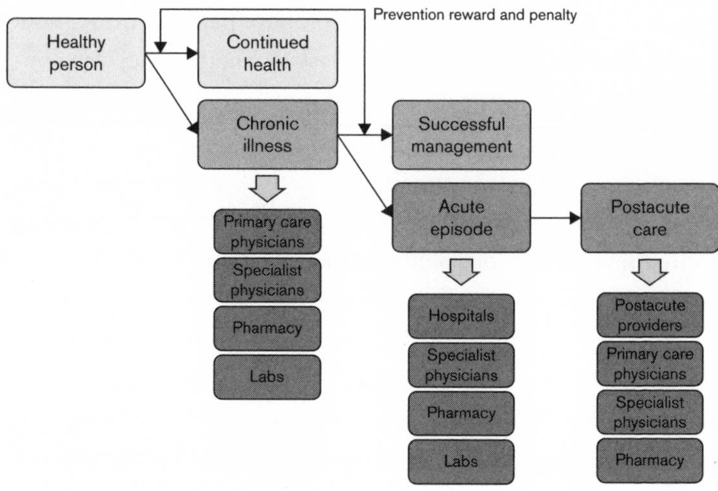

Figure 22. Primary care management. A system of primary care management would reward primary care providers for keeping patients healthy and managing chronic disease.

To increase integration across primary and specialty care, we can go even farther. The payment system might simply give all providers a fixed amount to care for a patient for a year. The providers involved in the payment arrangement could then work out how to jointly manage each patient and how to split the money. An example of such a payment system is shown in figure 23. An organization would agree to provide all the patient's care for a year. The more effectively the providers could prevent high-spending episodes, the better they would do financially. This is the model under which Kaiser operates, and it is increasingly the model for many large provider groups.

Together, bundled episode payments, primary care management payments, and patient-based payments are often known as "alternative payment systems." A number of insurers and medi-

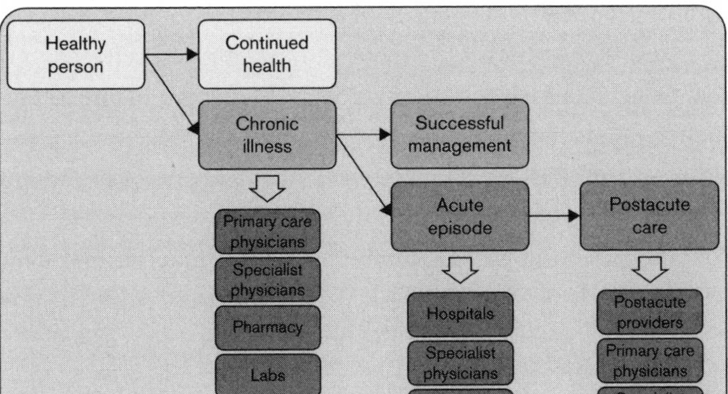

Figure 23. Patient-based payment. A patient-based bundled payment would group together all the services used by a patient over the course of a year. Providers in such a system would need to manage primary care and acute care services well.

cal care organizations are experimenting with payment systems like these as a way to encourage more cost-efficient care.

In practice, these systems often have one additional wrinkle: to reinforce the idea that quality matters too, not just cost savings, most alternative payment models make reimbursement dependent on measures of quality. For example, the system might specify a target for patient spending for the year (say $5,000) and a set of quality metrics, such as whether diabetic patients receive their recommended screening or a low rate of hospital readmission for patients with specified diagnoses. If the provider organization has realized costs below the spending target, they are eligible for a share of the gains. For example, if their actual spending is $4,000, they are eligible for up to $1,000 in bonus payments. The actual amount of the bonus they ultimately receive depends on their performance on the quality metrics. If they hit all the metrics, they might receive $600 in bonus payments. If their quality is average, they might receive half as much. If quality is poor, they might not receive any bonus or even suffer a loss. Thus providers can make money only by keeping costs low and quality high.

Of course, there are a number of issues and concerns about each of these payment models. Let me address in detail how each model might work and the problems that might arise.

• • •

Let's start with episode-based payment. A patient suffers a heart attack and needs treatment for a period of time to manage the condition and restore cardiac functioning. Since most specialists receive training in how to provide care throughout an episode, they can envision being responsible for managing the patient during the entire episode. Thus a group of cardiologists—in conjunction with the hospital where they practice—are in a natural position to manage the patient's episode. In terms of financing, the hospital and physician group together would receive a payment from the insurer, agree to provide some care themselves, and work out arrangements with other providers to fill in where they cannot. All care associated with the episode would come out of the episode total, even if there is a substantial adverse event and the patient requires additional care.

The obvious first question is how to determine payment for the episode. There are several approaches to this question. Some experts advocate starting with the care that ought to be provided during an episode and paying based on that amount. For example, one might determine the testing, surgical interventions, and medications that are necessary for heart attack treatment and its follow-up, and then price them out to determine the appropriate reimbursement. The Prometheus payment system does exactly this for a number of conditions; its evidence-informed case rates are currently being piloted in a number of areas.[17]

But this model makes many people uneasy. Who determines what care should be provided to each patient? One can imagine endless fighting over this. I worry about setting up a system with a built-in adversarial dynamic.

A second approach, which avoids the adversarial relationship, is to use current payment amounts as the base for a bundled payment. For example, the average cost of a heart attack episode is currently about $25,000. The insurer would start by converting that amount into a bundled payment, perhaps taking some off for likely efficiency gains, and transfer the total to the relevant provider group. Money would be saved both by lowering spending initially and by limiting the increase in the payment bundle over time.

Along with a colleague, Kaushik Ghosh, I have done an analysis of how such a payment system would work. Our calculations suggest that this type of system is quite manageable and could save a great deal of money.[18] Ghosh and I looked at medical claims for Medicare beneficiaries in 2007. We defined an episode by a hospital admission. Consider, as an example, a heart attack hospitalization. When a patient is hospitalized with a heart attack, an episode of care starts. We took the initial admission and added in all the claims for cardiovascular disease delivered to the patient in the next half year. For example, if there was a recurrent heart attack, that spending showed up in the original heart attack episode. If there was a subsequent hospitalization for a different condition, however—for example, surgery for colorectal cancer—a new episode was started. People could, and many did, have multiple episodes going on simultaneously. But a cardiologist would never be responsible for the cost of cancer care, and vice versa for an oncologist.

The system we came up with encompasses much of Medicare spending. About half of Medicare spending falls into one of the episodes we created; the remainder includes such services as screening mammograms and regular physician visits, for which there is no prior hospitalization. Further, spending is highly concentrated into a few episodes. The top seventeen episodes account for half of episode-associated spending, and the top forty-three account for three-quarters. This means that even modest forays into bundled episode payments could produce significant cost savings.

The episodes associated with the most Medicare spending are shown in figure 24. Osteoarthritis is the largest dollar cost; the primary spending here is for elective hip and knee replacements, which are increasing rapidly in volume. A variety of cardiovascular conditions are also high on the list, including coronary atherosclerosis and other heart disease, congestive heart failure, heart attacks, and heart valve disorders. No individual cancer represents a large enough share of spending to make it into the very top group, but cancer as a whole is a high-cost condition. Overall, episodes focused around musculoskeletal, cardiac, and to a lesser extent oncology services are the conditions with the highest price tags.

We then gauged the potential for cost savings in each of these areas. To judge this, we looked at the variation in spending in different parts of the country. We started by dividing the country into 306 regions within which medical treatments tend to be fairly similar.[19] For each area, we calculated average spending on

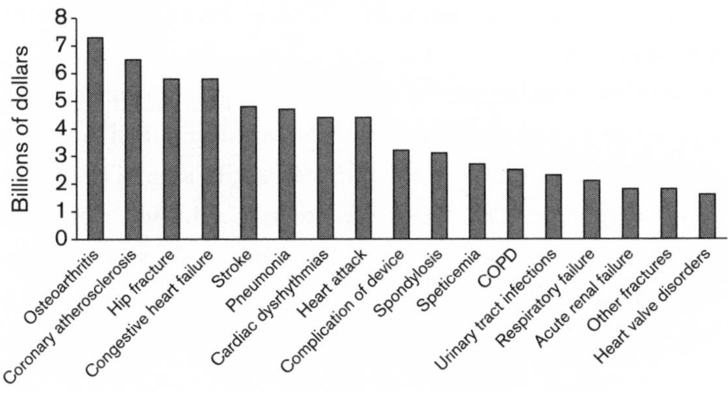

Figure 24. Episodes with the highest Medicare spending, 2007. Seventeen acute episodes account for half of episode-based spending. David M. Cutler and Kaushik Ghosh, "The Potential for Cost Savings through Bundled Episode Payments," *New England Journal of Medicine* 366 (2012): 1075–77, www.nejm.org/doi/pdf/10.1056/NEJMp1113361.

each episode. To the extent that the average spending differs across areas, it suggests that there are significant opportunities for savings. That is, in fact, what we found. In the case of osteoarthritis, for example, San Francisco, which falls in the seventy-fifth percentile of the spending distribution, spent 15 percent more than Jackson, Mississippi, which falls in the twenty-fifth percentile. Remember that this is spending for the same disease across a number of patients, so it is extremely unlikely to reflect differences in the severity of illness. Indeed, in the case of osteoarthritis, we can say more about what this variation involves. In high-spending areas, there were on average 1.3 hospital admissions per episode; in low-spending areas, it was closer to 1.1. In high-spending areas, $9,000 was spent on rehabilitation per case; in low-spending areas, rehabilitation spending was 30 percent less.[20]

To put a number on the potential savings, we calculated the amount that costs would be reduced if spending in all areas fell to the amount in the twenty-fifth percentile area. The savings were significant. For these seventeen conditions alone, the annual savings to Medicare from reducing costs by this amount would be $10 billion. There would be an additional savings to beneficiaries in reduced cost sharing and lower Part B premiums. Across all the episodes we identified, the savings from more efficient care would be 7 percent of total Medicare costs.

Our data clearly show the potential for savings from better management. But is there any evidence that providers can manage care in such a way as to achieve these savings? The answer is yes.[21] The Medicare program has engaged in several demonstrations of bundled episode payments, and each one has been successful. Medicare ran the first of these demonstrations in the early 1990s. The focus was on heart bypass surgery. Seven organizations were chosen to receive a bundled payment for bypass surgery, covering preoperative care, surgery, and postoperative care in the hospital and at the surgeon's office (note that they did not include postacute care in the bundle, thus reducing possible savings). The sites participating in the demonstration were geographically diverse. In all sites, four types of physicians were involved (thoracic surgeons, cardiologists, anesthesiologists, and radiologists), and they divided the payments with the hospital and any other physicians who saw the patient.

According to an independent evaluation, all seven of the sites saved money.[22] The savings ranged from 6 to 23 percent; the average was 10 percent. Further, this was done without any adverse outcomes; outcomes at the demonstration areas were in line with prior outcomes in those areas. Interviews with the administrators of the programs highlighted how they achieved the savings: encouraging greater involvement by surgeons in postoperative care, standardization of supplies and protocols (think of the Geisinger model), substitution of less expensive drugs for more costly ones, and engaging nurses in care management. All of this is basic, but it didn't happen without the bundled payment.

The success of the heart bypass demonstration pushed Medicare further into experimentation with bundled care arrangements. There was a demonstration for bundled cataract surgery payments that ran but was never properly evaluated, as well as planned demonstrations for cardiac and orthopedic care that never got off the ground. By about 2009, though, Medicare was back in the bundling business. In 2009, Medicare launched the Acute Care Episode demonstration. This program implemented a bundled payment for several cardiac and orthopedic procedures at five health systems located predominantly in the South and Southwest. The procedures chosen were relatively common: bypass surgery, joint replacement, and the like. Again, the bundle included only care for the inpatient episode; no post-acute care was involved.

Though the demonstration is ongoing, results to date are encouraging. Significant savings are being achieved (Medicare administrators expect 1 to 6 percent),[23] and the providers are comfortable with the organizational changes required—after overcoming their initial skepticism. At Baptist Health System in San Antonio, Texas, for example, the hospital has netted $8 million from the program, and the surgeons have pocketed $1 million.

To get these savings, providers had to reorganize the way they did business. Baptist, for instance, enacted a new compensation system for surgeons, with targets for quality and standardization around key supplies. Not all doctors liked this; at the Baptist site, four physicians left before the program was implemented. Still, the savings were achieved with the remaining physicians, and the surgeons at Baptist are comfortable with the way it has played out. According to the chief development officer at Baptist, "It wasn't a home-run. But I'd call it a solid triple."[24]

As a result of these demonstrations and countless studies of practice changes, there is little doubt among researchers that moving to bundled episode payments will save money. The Medicare program has indicated its interest in exploring this direction. As part of the Affordable Care Act, Congress authorized Medicare to conduct broader bundled payment demonstrations, including some focused on postacute as well as acute care. Medicare officials are starting down this path.[25] In the first iteration of the demonstration program, more than five hundred organizations volunteered to participate—an immense outpouring.

Truthfully, though, no further demonstrations are needed. We know how such systems work and what it takes to put them in place. What is needed is not another demonstration but a rapid transition from the existing fee-for-service payment model to bundled payment for episodes of care. Given the importance of cardiac and orthopedic care in high medical spending and the successes demonstrated with bundled payment for these conditions, the obvious place to start is bundling cardiac and orthopedic care. With appropriate legislation, Medicare could rapidly move to a national bundled payment system in those areas. These bundled payments could then be extended to other conditions, including the bulk of acute care. Private insurers could do this even without legislation; a number of private insurers are already moving down this path.

Specialists are ready for it. A 2011 survey by the Advisory Board Company found that while just 16 percent of hospital executives said they had bundled payments in place, 75 percent expected to have them by 2013, particularly from Medicare.[26] There is no reason not to meet this expectation.

• • •

An alternative to paying by the episode is to pay a fixed amount for the patient as a whole, covering all the care a patient will need in a year. This avoids the problem of determining what is part of an episode; when money follows the patient as a whole, everything is included in one reimbursement.

The idea of a patient-based payment system has a long history in health care. Many of the good organizations we have seen—Kaiser, for example—operate on a patient-based payment system and have done so for decades. In the 1990s, the term for this type of payment was "capitated payment," although this terminology has fallen out of fashion (along with the Backstreet Boys and the Spice Girls). Today, people focus more on the nature of the organization accepting such payments than on the specific payment it receives. An organization that accepts a global payment for a person for some period of time is termed an accountable care organization or ACO—though other names persist: a health bill in Oregon called them coordinated care organizations (CCOs). They have also been called integrated care organizations (ICOs). Virtually any three-letter acronym will do.

An accountable care organization looks very different from the current medical care system. Here primary care physicians and specialists must work together, and there must be a smooth flow between care settings. For this reason, establishing such organizations is complex.

The Affordable Care Act moved significantly to empower accountable care organizations. It directed Medicare program administrators to start such an accountable care organization program by January 2012 (less than two years after the bill was passed). The Medicare program created two models for these organizations. The first is for organizations like Kaiser, which are prepared to accept one payment per patient and assume all the spending risk for that patient. These are termed pioneer accountable care organizations. The second model is for organizations that are willing to assume some, but not all, risk. This is called the shared savings model. Such organizations share in some, but not all, of the savings from reduced costs.

Medicare has tried several demonstrations along these lines in the past, though none as large as the current program. To date, the experience is mixed. It is clear that there are high-performance organizations and lower-performing organizations, and that the better-performing ones are generally structured like accountable care organizations. Many of those organizations have been described in this book. What is less clear is whether lower-performing organizations can transform themselves into higher-performance ones as the payment model changes.

Several demonstrations conducted by the Medicare program suggest that this makeover is difficult. From 2005 to 2010, Medicare ran a physician group practice demonstration that enrolled ten physician groups in a shared savings model. The groups were paid on a fee-for-service basis but received performance bonuses if total spending fell by at least 2 percent and clinical quality met thresholds. The bonus was up to 80 percent of the savings. As usual, the groups were scattered throughout the country, though largely based in northern states.

The good news is that quality in the target settings was outstanding. On average, the medical groups met 98 percent of the quality measures set out by Medicare. This reflected hard work within the organizations. The bad news is that costs were not significantly affected. Several groups met the 2 percent savings target, but most did not. And the ones that met the target were unable to exceed it by substantial margins. The net savings to Medicare were small.

A more optimistic assessment of global payments comes from a recent experiment conducted in Massachusetts. Starting in 2009, Blue Cross Blue Shield of Massachusetts transitioned its payment methodology for a number of provider groups to a global payment model, termed the Alternative Quality Contract (or AQC, yet another three-letter acronym). In the AQC, enrolling groups of providers are given a per-capita spending target for each year, extrapolated from their own base-year spending and the typical growth rate of costs. Provider groups in the program are then benchmarked relative to this amount, benefitting from cost saving and suffering from cost overruns. In addition, high quality provides a second way to earn a bonus.

Seven physician organizations, accounting for more than one-quarter of Blue Cross Blue Shield patients, were enrolled in the program in the first year; an additional four organizations entered in the second year. Since Blue Cross Blue Shield is the largest private insurer in Massachusetts, this is an enormous part of the medical system.

Results from the first two years of the Alternative Quality Contract have now been published.[27] To date, the program has been very successful. In the first year, costs fell nearly 2 percent. In the second year, they fell even more. Ten of the eleven participating groups received a cost bonus in the second year. Some of the savings reflect lower utilization of expensive services, such as imaging; in other cases, primary care providers saved money by referring patients to less expensive specialists and admitting at less expensive institutions. Switching hospitals came with significant savings.

The high-priced institutions were obviously upset by losing patients. In response, some of the high-priced health systems in Massachusetts have asked insurers to lower the amount they receive as reimbursement so that they can compete for referrals.[28] (When is the last time anyone in health care asked to be paid less?) They are also joining the Alternative Quality Contract.

The savings from the Alternative Quality Contract did not come at the expense of quality. Quality rose in the participating organizations. Indeed, all eleven organizations earned a second-year quality bonus. The program is thus a resounding success and is being expanded rapidly.

It is not entirely clear why the Alternative Quality Contract resulted in large savings while the earlier Medicare demonstration did not. Part of the difference may be that prices paid by private insurers vary more across providers than the prices that Medicare pays. Thus there is a response to the private insurance program—switching to less costly providers—that is not viable for physicians participating in the Medicare demonstrations. In addition, the Alternative Quality Contract involved more provider groups that were less integrated to begin with. For these organizations, there was much more low-hanging fruit to be plucked in terms of basic care management and coordination. In contrast, most of the participants in the Medicare demonstration had already made investments in care management. Finally, the Alternative Quality Contract took place at a time of serious discussion about the need for cost savings in medical care, and the provider groups that joined the policy were intensely focused on cost savings. The Medicare demonstration program, in contrast, was seen as more of a quality improvement initiative than a cost reduction initiative. Whatever the reason, the Alternative Quality Contract results show that it is possible for organizational performance to improve and that global payment models encourage this improvement.

As noted above, the Affordable Care Act allows all health care organizations to have the opportunity to become accountable care organizations. Some analysts expected that there would be a wave of ready participants, and then enrollment would stall. In fact, just the opposite has occurred. Over 250 organizations have become accountable care organizations, and they now cover more than four million Medicare beneficiaries.[29] Changes by state Medicaid directors and private insurers imitating the Alternative Quality Contract could push the market even further. Thus a good share of the health care market may come under such payment models in the next few years.

• • •

The area of most experimentation in payment reform has been establishing pay for performance systems in primary care. In such a system, if the primary care practice can keep patients healthy and manage their chronic disease better, the practice gets paid more.

Although programs for primary care management differ, a typical program might begin by identifying measures of good prevention and chronic disease care based on the clinical literature. Common examples include ensuring that diabetics receive regular eye and cholesterol screens, women receive mammograms on schedule, and colonoscopy screens are conducted at recommended intervals. Primary care physicians are then offered a bonus plan: if they achieve high scores on these measures of care management, they will be paid a performance bonus, generally on the order of a few percent of revenue. The insurer monitors progress toward the goals using claims information submitted by the physician group. At the end of the year, an accounting is made, and payments are dispersed. Insurers have found it straightforward to implement this type of program because the measures of good performance are clear (they are often based on guidelines from professional societies), and the performance of the provider system is relatively easy to monitor (whether a test has been conducted can be readily determined).

A recent study reviewed 128 experiments focused on these types of pay-for-performance initiatives.[30] The results clearly indicate that clinical quality improves under these programs. Cancer screening rates increase (e.g., breast screening and colonoscopies), and rates of medication adherence rise. The improvement is often significant but not overwhelming. Interestingly, focusing on some elements of good care does not distract from other areas; paying more for good care for diabetic patients does not reduce the amount of care that nondiabetics receive, for example. Instead, quality increases even in areas not targeted by the performance payment.

Less fortunately, the interventions rarely save money. Providing better diabetes care reduces the number of diabetic-related heart attacks, but many people are treated and few heart attacks are prevented in any year. Hence, the system costs slightly more as a whole, at least in the period during which the programs have been evaluated.

The lack of cost savings does not mean the intervention is bad—improving health at low cost is always good—but it suggests that the cost savings from implementing only performance-based payment for primary care is likely to be limited. Most experts believe that primary care incentive programs need to be coupled with episode-based care for specialists or wrapped into a global payment for the patient as a whole, as with the Alternative Quality Contract.

• • •

One way or another, payment systems for medical care are likely to change markedly in the next few years. The long-established fee-for-service reimbursement model has run its course, and there are proven alternatives waiting in the wings. My guess is that payments will change substantially within the next five years, and the fee-for-service system will be largely gone within a decade. Based on the evidence above, I am optimistic that this reform will contribute to a higher-quality, lower-cost health care system.

In a time of optimism, though, it is important to consider what might go wrong. While there are many possible stumbling blocks, two strike me as particularly salient. First, there is a need to synchronize the changes occurring across the system. If every insurer decides on a new payment system without regard to what other insurers are doing, we could have a mess: doctors paid on a fee-for-service basis by some insurers, on an episode basis by others, and on a patient basis by still others. Each of these payment systems may be fine on its own, but putting them together does not work. It would be like a symphony orchestra in which the violin section is playing Mozart, the cellos are playing Beethoven, and the conductor is giving cues to Bach. The result would be a terrible cacophony.

Most market participants are looking to Medicare to take the lead in payment reform, as it has with so many other payment innovations (recall the Prospective Payment System discussed earlier in the chapter). With the debate about the constitutionality of the Affordable Care Act settled and President Obama remaining as president, further transformation of Medicare is certainly possible. But the danger is that Medicare policy will be stymied by legislative disagreement. Where Medicare has launched demonstration programs, we need to move beyond these demonstrations. Republicans who are hostile to the Affordable Care Act may not allow such changes legislatively, however, leaving Medicare stuck. If Medicare policy is gridlocked, or even goes backward, the entire movement will suffer.

In place of federal action, we may see action at other levels. The Massachusetts experience is encouraging along these lines. The fact that a private insurance company started the Alternative Quality Contract suggests that such innovation is not impossible. Indeed, big insurers in other states have made commitments to payment reforms that are similarly innovative.

Alternatively, state governments may become the leaders. With their large Medicaid and state employee spending on health care, state governments have an enormous say in the structure of the local medical care system. Recent legislation in several areas of the country shows the possibilities for state action. In Arkansas, legislation passed in 2011 requires Arkansas Medicaid and private insurers to implement bundled payment systems for five conditions: perinatal care, total joint replacement, and congestive heart failure are among them. Doctors are rewarded for quality and penalized for utilizing more services than their peers. The state plans to add many more conditions in the next few years, along with a comprehensive patient-centered medical home program.[31]

In Oregon, Medicaid changes implemented in 2012 spurred the creation of coordinated care organizations (CCOs), groups of providers that agree to care for the physical and mental health conditions of their beneficiaries. In exchange for an up-front investment by the state, the CCOs accept a global payment from the state, which grows less rapidly than cost increases under the prior system.[32] In this way, costs are reduced over time. Although the program was started only in the summer of 2012, fifteen CCOs were certified by the fall.

Perhaps the biggest changes are occurring in my home state of Massachusetts. Legislation passed in the summer of 2012 strongly encourages the transition to "alternative payment models."[33] The transition is required in public sector programs (Medicaid and state employees) and encouraged in private insurance. Given this new legislation and the ongoing Alternative Quality Contract, there is unlikely to be any significant presence of fee-for-service payment in the state within a few years.

These states are the farthest along, but several more states are considering or implementing legislation that addresses health care payment systems. Payment reform may thus become the province of state policy.

The second concern is about the capacity of providers to operate under a global payment system. Coordinating across the multitude of different providers is tricky business. Some organization has to manage payments, integrate IT systems, ensure cooperation among different physicians, and manage patient satisfaction. Who will be in a position to do all this? Almost by definition, none of the existing siloed providers is large enough to do it: primary care physicians control only a slice of the care their patients receive, and specialists only see patients when they are referred.

One common thought is that hospitals will run large care organizations. Many hospitals have long-standing relationships with physicians, often extending to owning their practices. In addition, hospitals have the financial acumen to negotiate bundled payments. It is no surprise that hospitals are now expanding rapidly and forming relationships with other hospitals, community physicians, and postacute care providers.

The difficulty with a hospital-run organization, however, is that the hospital is not particularly valued in a global payment model. In a setting of patient-based payment, the *least* efficient way to treat a patient is to admit him or her to a hospital. Physicians' offices and even homes are far more inviting. Imagine, then, the conflict when an expensive hospital owns a physician practice, and the physicians in that practice realize they can make more money on their global payment contract by avoiding the hospital entirely. The discussion will not be pleasant. To address this, hospitals are beginning to think of themselves as *health systems* rather than inpatient institutions. If these health systems are to run bundled payment systems, the transition from a hospital system to a health system will have to be a meaningful one.

More likely, many of these bigger organizations will be run by groups of physicians. Hospitals will be an input into care systems, but only one input; doctors will wield the real power. Indeed, economics tends to argue for this outcome. In any market, the people who ultimately wind up on top are the ones who provide the essential input—the technical skill that cannot be duplicated or the knowledge base that is unrivaled. That is far more commonly the physician than the hospital.

How physicians will come to be the organizers of care is not clear, though. Physicians are not trained as managers of big corporations, and there is no reason to expect that a single physician or even a group of physicians together can manage one of the most complex businesses in the economy. Thus, some type of management company will have to be invented to pool physician talent and organize an extremely complex production process. The group that is able to do that will provide a very valuable service—and probably make a good deal of money.

One issue I do not worry about is the common concern that this model is just a return of health maintenance organizations. HMOs (again, three letters!) were all the rage in the early 1990s. HMO insurers promised to deliver big savings to firms buying health care. They would do this by managing the care that people received (hence the synonym *managed care*) such that cost-effective care was provided and care that was not cost effective was left out. Concerned by the very high level of medical spending and its rapid growth, virtually all large firms moved their employees from open-ended reimbursement arrangements in the early 1990s to HMOs by the late 1990s (figure 25).

The transition to managed care was rapid and stunning. But the demise was even more rapid and even more stunning. After several years of straining against the rules imposed by managed care insurers, physicians and patients revolted. The managed care backlash was typified by the 1997 movie *As Good As It Gets,* in which the Helen Hunt character unleashed a flurry of expletives about managed care, and audiences across the country cheered loudly.

As the managed care era wore on, doctors and patients called for restrictions on what HMOs were able to do. Legislation was introduced for a Patients' Bill of Rights, but never passed. To a great extent, this was because firms buying insurance got the message and forced the insurance plans they contracted with to

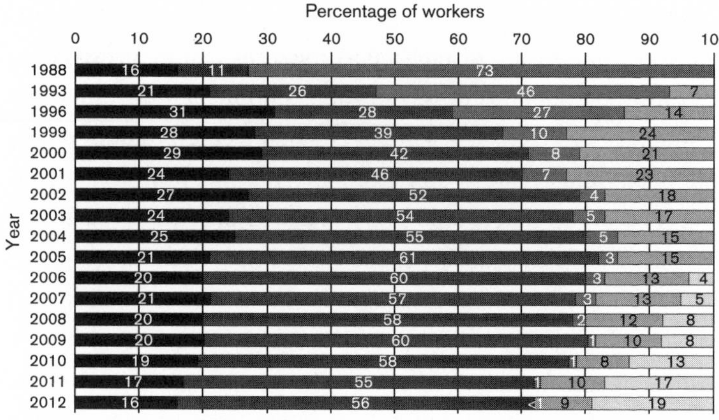

Figure 25. Distribution of health plan enrollment for covered workers by plan type, 1988–2012. I added 0.2% to each category (HMO, PPO, etc.) for 2007, 2009, and 2010 to make percentages sum to 100. Totals of the data for 1999, 2002, and 2012 are just above 100 percent. Chart adapted from Kaiser Family Foundation/Health Research and Education Trust, *Employer Health Benefits, 2012* (Washington, DC: Kaiser Family Foundation, 2012), http://kff.org/private-insurance/report/employer-health-benefits-2012-annual-survey.

be more lax. By the early years of the new century, HMOs were in decline, and patients were enrolled in much more open-ended plans (termed preferred provider organizations, or PPOs).

While some think of this as a warning sign about the global payment push, I do not. The global payment model is fundamentally different from the HMO model. In an HMO, insurers dictate to doctors and patients what they are allowed to do and what they cannot. Thus the insurer makes the decision about whether a referral is permitted, whether a hospitalization is authorized, or which medication should be used. Few doctors enjoy being dictated to.

In the global payment model, in contrast, physicians decide on good care and work with patients to provide that care. Thus the physician group makes decisions about which treatments to provide, which medications to use, and what testing to do. When physicians make decisions on the basis of their own reading of the evidence, they feel much more comfortable about the treatment. As Andrew Dreyfus, president and CEO of Blue Cross Blue Shield Massachusetts and the creator of the Alternative Quality Contract, said: "If we continue to be successful [in the AQC model], it will be physicians persuading other physicians that this liberates them and allows them to practice the kind of care they went into medicine to practice."[34] Indeed, in the successful models that have been presented, the physicians are in charge of designing appropriate care processes, monitoring the literature for what is necessary, and ensuring adherence to best standards. So when physicians talk to their patients, the advice they are giving is their own.

So it will have to be in these new payment arrangements. The cardiology managers in charge of heart attack episodes will have to involve physicians in designing care protocols, ensuring that the best care is provided, and upholding the integrity of the doctor-patient relationship. This is a difficult task, and it comes back to the fundamental concern noted above: what does it mean for an individual doctor to manage and work in a high-performance health care system? After all, that is the real heart of delivering good care. It is where we need to go.

CHAPTER SEVEN

Take Me to Your Leader

November 2000 was not a good month for the Obstetrics Department at Beth Israel Deaconess Medical Center in downtown Boston. BIDMC, as it is known, is a major teaching center that delivers about five thousand babies per year. That month, "Suzanne" was admitted to have her labor induced. Suzanne was a married, generally healthy thirty-eight-year-old expecting her first child. She had mildly elevated blood pressure, and her baby was at forty-one weeks gestation.[1] Because of the mild hypertension, Suzanne's doctor thought induction was the best course.

Suzanne's case seemed routine but ended up being tragic. After administration of a labor-inducing drug at 10:00 P.M., Suzanne was sent home (against guidelines, given her high blood pressure). She returned at midnight with even higher blood pressure. By 5:30 A.M., there were signs of an abnormal fetal heart rate. A cesarean delivery should have been performed but was not. At 6:10 A.M., delivery was attempted with forceps, but that too failed. At 6:30 A.M., an emergency cesarean delivery was performed. Unfortunately, the baby was stillborn.

Suzanne's woes continued. Her uterus had ruptured, and she was bleeding. She had a hysterectomy and spent three weeks in the hospital—most of it in intensive care. She survived, but her personal recovery took several years and she was unable to bear children. Suzanne and her husband ultimately adopted a child.

Suzanne's case is, sadly, typical of medical errors in the United States. But the hospital's response to the mistake was not. Rather than punishing individual physicians and carrying on as usual, the BIDMC decided to reevaluate its entire approach to obstetrical care. As it examined Suzanne's case, it realized that the failures went much deeper than a poor decision here and there. Rather, the system itself was at fault. Communication across physicians and between medical personnel and the family was poor. Treatment plans were not developed or properly adhered to. There was no standard for when to act when labor was not progressing as imagined. The busy obstetrics unit was unable to cope with heavy demand. The attending physician had been on call for twenty-one hours and was suffering fatigue. These were the root problems of the failure, and these were what BIDMC decided to fix.

Changing the culture and practice of an organization takes enormous time and effort. To fix the situation, the BIDMC turned to the Department of Defense. The Defense Department has significant experience in building functional teams; long ago, it figured out that poor teamwork was the cause of most military accidents.[2] With the help of the Department of Defense, the BIDMC introduced a Crew Resource Management (CRM) program in labor and delivery.

CRM is a technique to improve safety in complex situations where employees work in a hierarchy (a flight deck or a delivery room). Experts studying airline crashes frequently noted that first officers and flight engineers had attempted to bring critical information to the captain's attention before a crash (e.g., "Captain, we appear to be low on fuel"), but their comments were indirect and ineffective. By the time the information was conveyed, it was too late. Thus were born the goals of CRM: communication, situation monitoring, mutual support, and leadership. The idea is for the team to work together to solve a difficult problem.

To implement CRM at the Beth Israel Deaconess Medical Center, all personnel in obstetrics first took four hours of classroom instruction to learn the basic principles. Three teams were developed. The core team consisted of the primary care providers in obstetrics—obstetricians, residents, anesthesiologists, and nurses. They were to meet at least once every shift to formulate clear plans for each patient. A coordinating team of senior physicians and nurses was responsible for staffing, workflow, conflict management, and communication. A contingency team was set up to respond to emergencies. During each shift, a coaching team, consisting of a physician and nurse, reinforced teamwork.

BIDMC pioneered the program in 2002. By 2007, it was clear that it was a huge success. Compared to the period before CRM implementation, adverse obstetric events decreased by 23 percent, and high-severity malpractice claims decreased by 62 percent.[3] The BIDMC obstetrics team was awarded a Patient Safety and Quality Award for their work, and the program has spread to other hospitals.

The turnaround at Beth Israel Deaconess Medical Center's obstetrics unit was unique both in its broad focus and in the willingness of all concerned to address the root problems. Benjamin Sachs, the then head of obstetrics, saw through the error in this one case to find the deeper failures. Paul Levy, the then CEO of the hospital, encouraged major changes.[4] The care providers made it their mission to do better. In short, the entire organization was involved in improving quality.

• • •

Organizations are collections of people. The important question for health care is this: how can groups of people best be organized to produce better outcomes at lower cost? To borrow from a recent editorial, organizational change is the third phase of health care reform.[5] Phase 1 is covering people, and phase 2 is reforming the payment model to encourage better care. Phase 3 involves organizations changing their internal structures to deliver higher-quality, lower-cost care. But how can they do it?

To answer this question, let's move from health care to other industries. The situation facing health care is not so different from the problems other firms have faced, so what has been learned elsewhere has direct applicability.

The central truth from economic analysis is that some firms have processes to utilize talent well and others do not. In short, there are good performers and bad ones. The good news is that the difference between good and bad performers is not a wholly different set of employees. At BIDMC, after all, the same staff was there before and after the organizational intervention. Rather, the differences have to do with how the organization defines its mission, measures what it does, trains its employees, and motivates them.

A survey initially developed by the consulting firm McKinsey highlights the differences between high- and low-performance firms. McKinsey surveys firms in different industries;

Performance Monitoring
• What is the patient's journey through a typical medical episode? How are improvements to management of this pathway brought about? • How standardized are clinical processes? What mechanisms are used to prevent mistakes (e.g., checklists, patient barcodes)? • How are problems found and fixed, and who is involved? • What quality indicators are used, how frequently, and who sees the data?
Target Setting
• What types of targets are set for the hospital and your specialty, and what is their motivation? • How are staff involved, and how are they performing compared to others? • How often do you fulfill these goals? • How are clinicians involved in achieving cost and performance improvements?
Incentives & People Management
• If one of your best nurses or clinicians wanted to leave, what would the hospital do? • How long is underperformance tolerated, and how difficult is it to terminate staff? • Do some staff somehow always avoid being fired? • What is the promotion and bonus system like, and how do senior managers show that they are interested in attracting and developing talented individuals?

Figure 26. A sample of health care survey questions. Nicholas Bloom et al., "Management Practices across Firms and Countries," *Academy of Management* 26, no. 1 (2012): 12–33. For details, see www.worldmanagementsurvey.org.

figure 26 shows the questions in the health care survey. All told, there are twenty-one specific questions grouped into three broad dimensions. In performance monitoring, the first dimension, a variety of questions target how the firm monitors what is done and then feeds that information back to the relevant employees. This includes patient flow processes, determining and revising protocols, and identifying and resolving problems. In the best hospitals, treatment protocols are known and used by all staff, patients are informed of expectations and kept abreast of changes, and management monitors adherence to the protocols.

Outside of health care, Toyota is a famous example of good operations management. In a Toyota plant, any worker can stop the production line to fix an error. The correction process is not complete until the error is fixed and the underlying problem is addressed. Spotting errors is encouraged; having them recur is a major sin.

Target setting is the second area. Good firms set tough but realistic targets that are binding and apply to the entire organization. The nature of the target varies with the firm. Many manufacturing firms stress minimal defects in their targets. Over 58 percent of firms in the 2011 Compensation Data Manufacturing and Distribution survey reported using the Six Sigma approach, a method designed to have fewer than 3.4 defects per one million operations.[6] In service industries, customer service is paramount, and good firms measure and reward it.

In health care, performance generally includes a heavy emphasis on clinical targets. A high-scoring health care organization would set a stretch target—for example, eliminating hospital-associated infections. Performance would be monitored in real time and fed back to all staff. Performance scores would be the subject of departmental assessments and reviews for senior leaders and individual clinicians. Most of the health care industry has long been lax on setting targets, as the continued prevalence of hospital-acquired infections attests.

Individual employee incentives are the third area. Good organizations hire and promote on the basis of performance. Underperforming employees are either counseled to improve or let go. Employee incentives include both financial and nonfinancial rewards, as well as performance-based promotion (as opposed to seniority). Money is one component; designing appropriate compensation systems is a central part of corporate activity. Public recognition is another. Firms from Nordstrom's to Zappos to Caesar's Entertainment are famous for their monetary and nonmonetary reward systems for employees.[7] The survey gets at this domain by asking how reviews are performed, salaries are set, and underperformers are addressed.

How does health care rank on these various dimensions? Economists Nicholas Bloom, John Van Reenen, and their colleagues have conducted management surveys on over ten thousand organizations internationally to measure performance in each of these three domains. Conducting these surveys is challenging, since all firms want to look good when asked about their management practices. When Bloom, Van Reenen, and their team survey firms, they have MBA-level students speak to middle managers—people in charge of a particular plant or service in the hospital (e.g., oncology)—and ask them open-ended questions about how the institution operates. They then code the responses on a five-point scale, 5 being the best possible score and 1 the worst. The average of the scores in the three areas is used to determine an overall score for the organization.

Bloom, Van Reenen, and their colleagues primarily survey manufacturing firms, though they have also surveyed several hundred hospitals (and a few schools). The sample includes organizations in the United States, the United Kingdom, Japan, Germany, and several developing countries.

Their data shows clearly that management practices differ across firms, and that firms with better scores do better.[8] In manufacturing industries, firms that score better in the survey have higher sales per worker, greater profitability, fewer bankruptcies or other exits, and more employees. In health care, hospitals with better scores have higher survival rates for heart attacks.

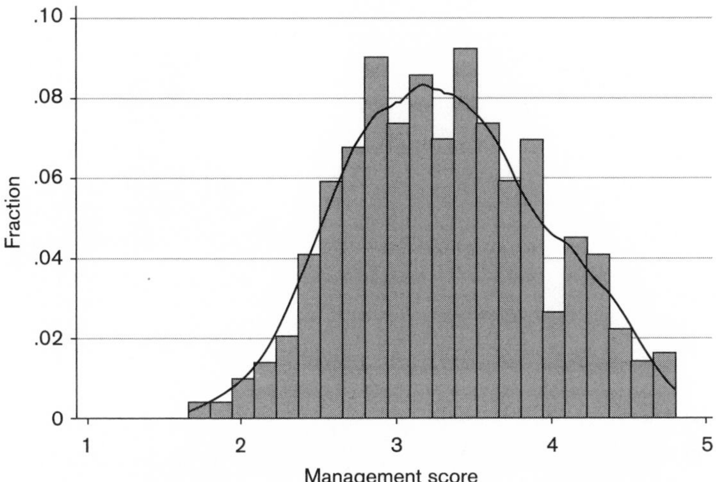

Figure 27. Management score distribution for U.S. manufacturing firms. Data are reported at www.worldmanagement.org. The solid line is the kernel density estimate.

Children attending schools with better management practices do better on standardized tests.[9]

They also find enormous variation in management practices across industries and countries. Figure 27 shows the distribution of management scores in U.S. manufacturing firms. The average U.S. manufacturing firm has a score of 3.35 on the five-point scale (1,196 organizations were surveyed). This is the highest of any country (Japan and Germany are tied for second at 3.23).

Hospital performance is more mixed (figure 28). On average, hospitals in the United States score much lower than manufacturing firms. The average hospital score is only 3.0, 0.35 point below the manufacturing average. Only 12 of the 610 hospitals (2 percent) score at least a 4.0, compared to 17 percent of manufacturing firms. The good news is that U.S. hospitals are better

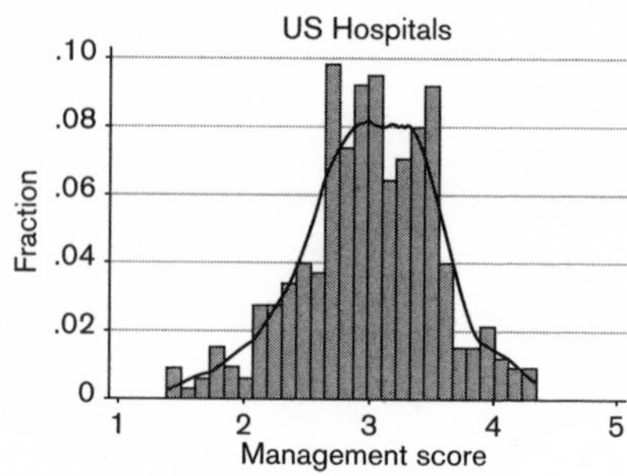

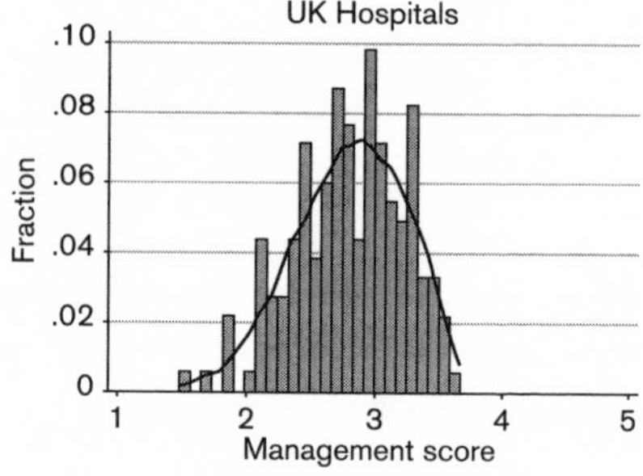

Figure 28. Management score distribution for U.S. and U.K. hospitals. Data are reported at www.worldmanagement.org. The solid line is the kernel density estimate.

managed than their international competitors. The average British hospital score is only 2.8.

American hospitals are low in all three areas of management, though somewhat better at performance monitoring than target setting and incentives. In the area of performance monitoring, U.S. hospitals average 3.2; the comparable score in manufacturing is 3.6. The score for target setting is only 2.9 (the manufacturing average is 3.3), and the score for incentives is also 2.9 (3.3 in manufacturing). Relative to these means, private hospitals score higher than public hospitals; the difference is appreciable. To put these numbers in perspective, note that the difference between the average hospital and the average manufacturing firm amounts to 4 percent greater profits or 2 percent fewer deaths per 100 patients with a heart attack.[10] It is clear that American hospitals will need to organize themselves and think differently about their mission in order to do better.

• • •

Performance measurement, target setting, and employee incentives are all important in running organizations. But special care needs to be taken as health care organizations change; it would be a big mistake to run a hospital the way outsourcing firms run manufacturing plants.

Perhaps the most important rule of health care management is this: *never put care providers in a position of denying care for financial reasons.* Physicians are ethically and legally bound to treat all patients in need, and they (rightly) rebel when they are told to ration. Thus good organizations do not put physicians in this position. In this sense, health care is very different from building a car. In the automobile industry, it is understood that not all customers are willing and able to pay for the most expensive products. Automobile workers do not feel guilty when they build a car that is less expensive but perhaps more vulnerable in a crash. In health care, doctors and nurses believe that all people should have the same chance to survive a crash.

The biggest implication of this rule is that guidelines for care providers should be based on medical effectiveness, not cost criteria. When Intermountain Health Care designs clinical pathways, its challenge to physicians is to produce the pathway that will lead to the best health outcome, not the episode of care with the lowest cost. Similarly, Kaiser decides which drugs and devices to use only after clinical efficacy has been assessed. Drugs and devices are traded off only when they are judged to have the same efficacy and side-effect profile. As a result, when a treatment choice is made, providers and patients in both systems are sure that they are providing the best possible care.

The issue of cost-effectiveness is so fundamental to the discussion that it deserves some expansion. All medical care has costs and health impacts. The question is how to account for both in deciding what to do. The easiest situation occurs when care is costly but delivers nothing; elective inductions of births before thirty-nine weeks gestation and back surgery for routine cases of lower back pain are two examples. In those circumstances, it is easy to decide that the unnecessary care should be eliminated.

However, there are other circumstances where care has some value, but that value is small relative to the cost. Take the example of Avastin, an antibody injected intravenously that inhibits the growth of tumors. Avastin is used to treat various types of cancers, including colorectal, lung, glioblastoma, and kidney. The manufacturing process for Avastin is complex. It uses Chinese hamster ovarian cells and the antibiotic gentamicin to express Avastin's active ingredient, bevacizumab.[11] Because Avastin is so expensive to make, it commands a high price; a standard course of therapy costs about $50,000.

Avastin extends survival for those with metastatic colorectal cancer, but not by much. Clinical trials have shown that patients receiving Avastin live on average 1.4 months longer than patients who do not. Thus, the cost-effectiveness of Avastin is $425,000 per additional year of life ($50,000/1.4 months). Often the quality of those months is not high. Should cancer centers putting together guidelines for the treatment of colorectal cancer include the possible use of Avastin?

If the patient is paying for significant parts of the treatment out of pocket, a physician might well recommend not using Avastin. Memorial Sloan-Kettering Cancer Center in New York, one of the finest cancer hospitals in the country, recently decided not to recommend the cancer drug Zaltrap for patients with advanced colorectal cancer, because the unreimbursed cost of the therapy was extremely high, and there was no good evidence of benefit relative to other treatments (ironically, in this case Avastin is the other treatment; Zaltrap costs twice as much as Avastin).[12]

When out-of-pocket costs are not an issue, however, the situation is trickier. Most economists argue against national health care programs covering Avastin for metastatic cancer because the cost is so high relative to the benefit (recall the threshold of $100,000 or less per year of additional life). Money spent on Avastin is not available for education, environmental protection, or other uses. If patients want Avastin, they would either pay for it out of pocket or buy supplemental insurance that covers Avastin and other therapies that do not pass standard measures of worth.

Some countries follow this logic. The National Health Service in the United Kingdom, for example, does not cover Avastin for the treatment of colorectal cancer.[13] Similarly, the prostate cancer drug Abiraterone was not approved for use until the manufacturer agreed to a discount.[14]

In the United States, however, we have walled off cost from coverage determinations. The Food and Drug Administration is prohibited from disapproving drugs because of their cost, and the Medicare program cannot refuse to cover a treatment for cost reasons.[15] Medicare and private insurers pay a lot for Avastin. Total spending on Avastin for metastatic colorectal cancer is unknown, but Avastin sales total about $3 billion annually.[16]

Many people worry about being rationed out of drugs like Avastin. Recall how people rebelled against HMOs largely because they thought they were being rationed by cost. And this concern was one of the most powerful complaints against the

Affordable Care Act. When that legislation was being drafted in 2009, those opposed to the plan made the issue of death panels a major public rallying cry—despite the fact that there weren't any in the law and none had ever been contemplated. Even after the law was passed, a government panel created to make Medicare payment changes more flexible became a group of "unelected bureaucrats empowered to cut Medicare."[17] It is unclear whether the body will ever come into existence.

Politicians who push these objections are clearly pandering to imperfectly informed individuals. But these examples highlight an important aspect of the public's views. Most people believe that medical care has so much pure waste—care with no medical benefit at all—that we should focus on that waste first and leave aside the ethically challenging questions about what to do with care that is marginally effective but very expensive. In the examples we have been discussing, people want to eliminate unneeded cesarean sections long before considering whether Avastin should be covered.

Given how much waste has been identified, this is not a crazy view. As we have seen, about one-third of medical spending is not associated with any health improvement. Further, eliminating this waste will require concentrated effort for some period of time. At some later point, we might need to consider whether Avastin is worth covering as a central benefit, but deferring this decision is reasonable.

• • •

There is a second rule about health care that will be important as medical organizations change their operations: *individual physicians should not be compensated based on the clinical outcomes of each patient.* This rule, too, is different from many other industries.

Before explaining why this is the case, recall the distinction between the organization and the individual. In the previous chapter, I argued that health care *organizations* should be paid on a performance basis. Here, I argue this should not be the case for the *individual physician*. For example, consider a cardiologist who works in a large cardiology practice. It is quite reasonable, and helpful, for the cardiology practice to be paid on a performance basis—if they have better outcomes, they should earn more. That is not true of the individual cardiologist, however.

To understand why this rule is important, let's start off with a counterexample where pay-for-performance works well. There are many examples of this, though one will suffice. Edward Lazear, a professor at Stanford Business School and the former chief economic advisor to President George W. Bush, conducted a study in the late 1990s on productivity in the auto glass industry.[18] His example was Safelite, the country's largest installer of automobile glass. In 1994 and 1995, Safelite moved from an employee compensation system based on hours worked to one based on productivity. In the new system, workers were paid per piece of glass installed; there was a minimum hourly wage but ample opportunity for speedy employees to increase their wages. The results of introducing performance-based pay were enormous. Productivity increased by 44 percent under the new system (output went from 2.7 panes installed per hour to 3.2 panes per hour). Worker pay rose as well.

One might worry that quality would fall with performance-based pay; being quick but sloppy allows a worker to move on to other jobs faster. However, because defects can be readily identified and attributed to specific workers (the glass will break shortly after installation), Safelite managed quality by having the worker who incorrectly installed the glass redo it with no additional compensation. The possible loss of income is a major incentive to do the job right, so overall quality improved under performance-based pay. The result was a win-win situation.

Performance-based pay has quietly become the norm in American industry. From teaching to retail to manufacturing, employers increasingly value work done well. Indeed, scholars defend the high pay of corporate CEOs in the United States by reference to the increasing performance incentives in their contracts (though many are unpersuaded).[19]

Why is there one rule for auto repair technicians and another for surgeons (human repair technicians)? The answer is that every patient is subtly different from other patients in ways that are not true of cars. Two patients may have similar clinical presentations but differ in cognitive capacity, ability to cope with surgery, presence of family supports, and other factors. The one that has more of these resources is likely to come through surgery better than the one that has fewer.

Paying individual doctors on the basis of their outcomes penalizes surgeons for taking cases that are more difficult, thus encouraging doctors to avoid such patients entirely. Without being able to specify exactly which part of the outcome was a result of the surgeon's performance and which was a result of patient idiosyncrasies, compensating surgeons on the basis of health outcomes creates disincentives to treat sicker patients.

The subtle differences among patients set health care apart from other industries. Two cars with a cracked window are virtually identical; two patients with the same condition rarely are. Thus, if one auto glass repair technician fixes a car in half as much time as a coworker, the first is clearly more productive. In contrast, if one surgical team has a death and a second does not, it does not necessarily mean that the second team practiced better care. The relationship between inputs (technical quality, team communication, and so on) and outputs (whether the patient lived or died) is more tenuous in health care than in other industries. At the level of the group, however, outcomes are more stable, and it is expected that subtle differences across patients wash out. Thus group outcomes (adjusted for observable risk) are a better guide to true quality than are individual outcomes.

How should quality factor into a physician's compensation? In a setting where outcomes are not definitively related to the quality of care, it makes more sense to compensate physicians on the basis of quality measures that we can observe—their surgical inputs and that of their team. Did they perform the preoperative assessment, surgery, and postoperative monitoring in the technically correct manner? Did the team interact appropriately? If so, the physician should get high marks, even if the outcome was unfortunate.

The good health care firms we observed have thought about this and adjusted their compensation systems accordingly. The Mayo Clinic, Kaiser Permanente, and other successful groups often pay physicians a salary. These organizations do not want physicians to provide more care than is necessary, so they do not pay them on a fee-for-service basis. They also do not want to penalize doctors for seeing sicker patients, to they avoid adjusting pay based on the outcome of specific patients.

Further, their nonfinancial rewards are all associated with providing better care, not just avoiding bad outcomes. Kaiser screens new physician hires for an interest in practicing in a closed group system like Kaiser's. A new physician practices for three years before making partner, during which time both sides ensure that the physician is comfortable and productive in the Kaiser model. Hiring and promotion at the Mayo Clinic is similar. Despite its ability to draw superstars, the Mayo Clinic does not want all superstars on its staff. It values fitting into the organization as much as clinical reputation.

Other organizations use a combination of salary and billable services. For example, Intermountain pays its physicians a salary supplemented by a performance bonus associated with patient volume. To counteract the incentives for overtreatment that result from the volume-based payment, Intermountain has an IT system to guide decision-making and encourages constant feedback from professional colleagues. In that sense, physicians at Intermountain see good care, not the size of their paycheck, as the driving force.

Importantly, at Kaiser, Intermountain, the Mayo Clinic, and like organizations, physicians earn about what they could outside of the organization. None of these organizations wants to employ only doctors willing to take a pay cut. But the doctors earn their money based on the quality of care provided and not how many services they bill.

• • •

The third rule about health care improvement is that it can and should involve more than just health care providers. *Patients have a lot to contribute to care improvement, and their voices should be heard.*

A crisis at Cincinnati Children's Hospital Medical Center (CCHMC) provides an example of this. CCHMC has a sterling reputation and a mandate to inform patients about everything. Imagine their consternation, then, when they found out in 2001 that their cystic fibrosis program was not up to par. Cystic fibrosis (CF) is a genetic disease that results in excess mucus forming in the lungs. In addition to hampering breathing, the mucus can lead to infections, which become antibiotic-resistant over time.

CF is life threatening. Average life expectancy for a child diagnosed with the disease is thirty-seven years—a massive improvement over the past (in 1962, life expectancy was ten years), but still not long. Thirty thousand adults and children in the United States have CF.[20]

CF cannot be cured, but it can be managed. The key elements in management include proactive treatment of airway infections (including use of antibiotics, breathing devices, and inhalation medication), good nutrition, and an active lifestyle. Because the course of the disease varies from patient to patient and significant time is involved in managing the disease, CF is typical managed by specialists at large, multidisciplinary centers. CCHMC was just such a center.

The Cystic Fibrosis Foundation collects details about quality at individual centers but for a long time did not release that data publicly. In the early 2000s, it did.[21] For the first time, organizations got a good look at how they were doing. CCHMC, a hospital that thought it was at the top of its game, learned that the lung functioning of its cystic fibrosis patients ranked at only the twentieth percentile of national performance.

CCHMC was horrified. Should they disclose the information to patients or try to correct the situation first? Rather than burying the finding or arguing that more study was needed (maybe their patients were sicker than other patients?), they decided to publicize the data. But then they communicated with patients. Did parents want to take their children elsewhere? If so, they would make it easy to do so, transferring records, medications, and histories.

To their surprise, not a single patient moved to another facility. Rather, they wanted to help. Families came forward with suggestions to help raise quality and improve the patient experience—both by addressing lung function and in other ways.

The parents wanted shorter clinic visits, more positive language regarding CF and their children (e.g., not describing children as "failures"), and a method for categorizing patients based on their needs—nutritional, antibiotic, and so on. The result was a thorough redesign of the cystic fibrosis clinic, using many of the principles we have discussed. By 2008, six years after the progress improvement initiative, CCHMC's patients had lung function at the ninety-fifth percentile of the national scale.[22] The involvement of families was a major reason.

• • •

Change in health care is necessary, but that does not make the transition any easier. No one likes the idea of having to restructure how they work—least of all professionals who put so much time and energy into their profession. Rather than brush by these fears, we need to address them.

Perhaps physicians' greatest fear regarding organizational change is that they will become "cogs in a wheel" rather than valued, independent professionals. "Cookie-cutter medicine" is the term for this. If physicians are just going to do what a computer says, what is the value of being a physician?

Ironically, the evidence demonstrates the opposite: physicians who practice with sophisticated information technology systems are not only more productive but happier as well. Information technology codifies the routine aspects of practice. Computers can be programmed to understand all the medication rules in a medical textbook. The computer can then remember those rules and do the equivalent of cutting the cookie the same way every time, thus ensuring that all patients with a particular condition are prescribed the right combination of therapies and receive the right tests. Physicians are needed for the hard parts: dealing with complex diseases where a single treatment path is not appropriate, guiding patients with a constellation of conditions that does not fit the textbook, operating on the human body, and interacting with human beings to help them deal with complex, life-changing decisions. In the end, this is the part of medicine that is the most difficult and the most rewarding.

Dr. David Blumenthal summed this up well. Blumenthal was my colleague in putting together the Obama health plan and went on to head of the Office of the National Coordinator for Health Information Technology from 2009 to 2011. He is also a practicing internist. About electronic medical records, Blumenthal recalled,

> When I started using an EHR, I found it challenging. I often longed for a dose of my old prescription pad (confession—I cheated once in a while). I chafed at reconciling medication lists, updating problem lists, scanning through seemingly endless consultant notes. (In the past, many wouldn't have been available—lost somewhere in the paper world.) It was much easier to use the triplicate x-ray requisition I had used for 30 years than the radiology order entry software required by my EHR. My visits were longer and more complicated. Every time I turned on the computer, it seemed, I had to learn something new. But I am glad I did it.... My EHR made me a better doctor. I *really* knew what was going on with my patients. I could answer their questions better and more accurately. I made better decisions. I felt more in control.[23]

Evidence shows this view to be widespread. In a 2008 study, 90 percent of physicians with EMRs were satisfied with it, and the vast bulk reported that the system improved the quality of care they provided.[24] Of course, these were the early adopters. I wondered if perhaps they had a particular affinity to computerized medicine. That does not appear to be the case, however. In a 2011 survey, 85 percent of physician adopters were satisfied with their EHR, and three-quarters thought it improved the quality of care.[25]

Physicians' fear that IT will take away their autonomy is no different than the fear of workers in many other industries.[26] Professionals from lawyers to authors to teachers have worried that information technology would turn them into automatons. The first disenfranchising technology was electricity; the computer is an extension of that. Clearly, this disenfranchisement happens in some cases. Electricity reduced the demand for candle makers, and computers eliminated the need for people whose sole job was to do tedious mathematical calculations by hand (the way the first atomic bombs were modeled).

But in most cases, fears of disenfranchisement have been wrong. In industry after industry, use of automation has increased the demand for highly educated workers and allowed them to do their jobs more productively. A lawyer can be better when he has the entire history of case law at his fingertips. That lawyer is more productive and earns more as a result. Medical researchers similarly benefit from easy access to data. The real skill of research involves analyzing data, not pulling data out of obscure studies. In these industries and more, technological change has led to increasing wages for skilled workers.

The same is likely to be true in medicine. Doctors will not need to be walking textbooks, but they will be needed to know when the textbook is useful and when to depart from it. And in those cases where the textbook is not an accurate guide, the doctor will need to be there monitoring the patient and making sure everything goes well.

Fear of losing earnings or status is not the driver for all physicians. Some physicians simply enjoy practice the way they have it and do not wish to learn new skills. When Virginia Mason went down the path of quality improvement, a handful of physicians left—they preferred a different type of practice.[27] Similarly, several surgeons left the Baptist Health System in San Antonio when that system accepted bundled payments for orthopedic surgery and wanted to standardize care processes. Turnover in these situations is often good for the organization: the remaining care providers are more dedicated to the mission and wind up happy. But it can be stressful.

Doctors end up being happy with change in part because they are so unhappy in the current system. In talking with countless physicians and nurses over the years, I have discovered a remarkable phenomenon: Health care providers are in one of the highest status professions in the country, and they make (literally) life-and-death decisions for the people they treat. Yet they are frustrated by their lack of autonomy. How can this be? The answer is that doctors and nurses have great autonomy over the individual *patient* they see, but they have essentially no control over the *system* they work in. The administrative system chokes them; the information they want is missing or hard to obtain; and they fear being sued for outcomes that are not their fault. How could they not feel frustrated?

When I talk to groups of medical personnel, I ask them two questions. First I ask, "Can you think of ways your institution can run more efficiently—so that costs would be lower and patient outcomes better?" Most people look confused when I pose this question (why is an economist asking me this?). But after the question sinks in, results come pouring forth: administrative systems could be streamlined; supplies could be properly maintained; service transfers could be more efficient. In no time at all, an audience of clinical personnel might generate over twenty good ideas.

I then ask, "Why haven't you made these changes?" This too catches people off guard. They stutter a bit and then give an answer akin to "Because no one has asked me." Physicians are one of the most skilled workforces in the country, with enormous brainpower and energy, and yet no one has asked them for basic suggestions about improving the way they work. An autoworker at a Toyota plant has more say in the operation of the assembly line than a doctor has in the operation of a hospital? That cannot be right.

• • •

"Of course there are things that are wasteful. I do them because it prevents a lawsuit." This statement, or something akin to it, is a view commonly expressed by physicians. It is usually followed by the suggestion that if society wants to have less wasteful medical care, it should limit lawsuits. Doctors are right on this: we do need to reform medical malpractice. But at the same time, we need to make the right reforms.

Our system for dealing with medical errors is founded on good intentions. If a patient experiences an adverse outcome resulting from negligence on the part of care providers, the patient (or the family) is entitled to compensation. There is nothing wrong with having such a rule. Compensation for harm is natural and beneficial.

The difficulty is how the rule is carried out. It is difficult if not impossible to determine when bad events are caused by medical care and when they occur randomly. Did the patient not recover from the surgery because of an error the surgeon made or simply because the patient was very sick? Courts do not find this determination easy—even more so when the death is heartbreaking. Thus winning or losing a malpractice case seems like a roll of the dice to physicians. And since some patients are bound to have bad outcomes, the probability that a doctor will be sued is very high. In the riskiest specialties (neurosurgery and thoracic-cardiovascular surgery), about 20 percent of physicians have a claim filed against them *each year*.[28] Over a lifetime, effectively all physicians in these specialties will be sued. Even in specialties with the lowest risk (family practice, psychiatry, and pediatrics), about 70 percent of doctors have a claim filed against them in their lifetimes. Just hiring lawyers and adjudicating claims absorb half the money paid in settlements and judgment awards.

And then there is defensive medicine. To avoid possible litigation, doctors do extra tests (such as ordering an MRI even for mild head trauma) and avoid some patients (like high-risk pregnant women). A variety of studies have estimated the magnitude of defensive medicine relative to total medical spending. Generally, these studies look at how physicians' practice differs among states that make it easier or harder to sue. Do physicians order fewer tests when laws make it harder to collect from doctors? The answer is yes—but the magnitudes are not large.

In one recent study, researchers estimated that reducing malpractice insurance premiums by 10 percent would result in a 0.2 percent savings in overall health spending.[29] The results make sense but the total savings is not great. Across a range of studies, defensive medicine has been estimated to account for about 2 percent of total medical spending.[30] To put the figure another way, if the federal government mandated that all states adopt the strictest tort reform rules in existence (used in California, Virginia, and Arkansas), medical spending would be projected to decline by 2 percent over the next decade—far less than the one-third of spending that is believed to be wasteful.[31]

What is perhaps more insidious than the cost of defensive medicine is the way the system makes physicians wary about admitting and learning from mistakes. Let's go back to Suzanne, the pregnant woman who suffered as a result of negligence at the Beth Israel Deaconess Medical Center. The response of many hospitals would be to deny that the medical personnel had made mistakes. Suzanne had an unfortunate outcome, but that was just the result of the disease process. The hospital did all it could to make it right.

Such a strategy might prevent a lawsuit and payout (along with admitting the mistake, BIDMC reached a financial settlement with the family). But if mistakes are not admitted, they cannot be fixed, and the underlying systems leading to those mistakes cannot be improved. Doing health care right requires learning from mistakes, and that can only happen if mistakes are brought into the open.

The irony is that admitting mistakes is not only better for improving the system but often better financially for the institution. In 2001, the University of Michigan Health System developed what it calls a disclosure-with-offer program. Any time providers believe they have committed an error or a complaint is filed, a full assessment is conducted. If the practitioners have indeed made a mistake, they apologize to the patient and their family and work with the parties harmed to reach a solution. If the health system concludes that correct clinical care was provided, this too is communicated to the patient. The difference is that disclosure is complete and settlement offers are made proactively rather than as a last recourse.

A recent study examined the impact of the disclosure-and-offer program on malpractice claims.[32] The study showed a remarkably favorable impact on the malpractice burden. Compared to pre-change values, the number of malpractice claims fell by one-third, lawsuits fell by two-thirds, and compensation declined by 60 percent. For many patients, honesty and the knowledge that the mistakes that affected their loved one will be fixed are enough. The University of Michigan program gives them this.

The Michigan results have led other health systems to adopt this model. Some states are now encouraging it as well, enacting legislation that allows providers to apologize for an error without that apology being used as evidence in court. Massachusetts recently endorsed the disclosure, apology, and offer process in its landmark health care cost legislation—the same legislation that proposed the bundled payment initiatives noted in the last chapter.[33]

Even still, there is a ways to go. Most physicians are still traumatized by the malpractice system—and they are right to feel that way. For this reason, malpractice reform needs to be a part of a better-functioning health care system. In his 2009 speech to the American Medical Association, President Obama recognized this: "And while I'm not advocating caps on malpractice awards which I believe can be unfair to people who've been wrongfully harmed, I do think we need to explore a range of ideas about how to put patient safety first, let doctors focus on practicing medicine, and encourage broader use of evidence-based guidelines."[34] The Affordable Care Act does not contain much in the way of malpractice reform, but it allocates $50 million for tort reform demonstration projects.

The area where the most experimentation could be done is in creating a tort exemption for medical practice consistent with clinical guidelines.[35] The idea is that doctors should have a presumptive defense if they followed the guideline and did not make errors in doing so (e.g., they performed surgery when the guideline indicated it, and there was no error during the operation). An evidence-based malpractice system would automatically dismiss claims that followed a recognized guideline, even if the actual outcome was not the sought-for outcome.

Various states have experimented with malpractice reforms that attempt to do this. Maine tried this type of demonstration in the 1990s, enacting a law that allowed physicians who adhered to best practices to use this as a viable defense should they be sued for malpractice.[36] In the brief experience with the Maine system (in effect from 1992 to 2000), there was no effect on the number of malpractice claims or the costs and premiums.[37] Indeed, no doctors used adherence to clinical guidelines as part of their defense. However, the demonstration in Maine was fairly narrow. Only four specialties were chosen for the demonstration, and as a result, only 1 to 2 percent of Maine's cases were affected. In addition, there were few practice guidelines widely used at the time. Partial reforms along these lines were also attempted in Florida and Minnesota, but again the evidence did not suggest major improvement.

It is not clear to researchers what should be done now. One group of analysts follows the money. The best evidence we have is that medical costs can be reduced when it is harder to collect from physicians and their insurers. Thus many adherents believe we should make collection for malpractice more difficult. The decrement to this approach is that it does not make the system better as a whole. Another group believes that we should use the malpractice system to incentivize good care and a learning health system. Beyond encouraging the Michigan model, however, we still do not know how best to design such a system. My inclination is to follow the latter approach and encourage better care and more rapid resolution of disputes. But I fully admit that we do not have the answer as yet.

. . .

Practicing better medicine cannot be mandated. The steps involved in organizational change are too detailed for any outside body to require. We can require hospitals to draw up plans to streamline operations, but just putting the labels on paper and changing the titles of some executives do not bring real change. Telling nurses they can challenge doctors who do not follow protocols is fine—until the first nurse gets yelled at for slowing down the physician, and her supervisor does not back her up.

In this regard, health care is not that different from other industries. Many firms have visited Toyota plants to learn about the Toyota production system; Toyota has been extremely generous about sharing its knowledge. A number of these firms have taken the Toyota method back home and tried to use it in their own factories. But those replications fail as often as they succeed. Even knowing exactly what Toyota does, firms cannot always imitate it. Real change requires an entirely new culture, not just the use of buzzwords.

Unfortunately, there is little that society can do to force this change. What we can do is set the stage for it. Where IT is lacking, the government can subsidize IT investments and require practices to become electronic. Where payments are based on doing more, the government can change its payment system to a new model. Where malpractice fears stifle high-quality care, we can intercede. And we can offer to help providers that want to do better. But as any psychologist will attest, the patient needs to be ready to change for it to occur.

CHAPTER EIGHT

How Long Will It Take?

Focusing on quality has the potential to fix much of what ails American medicine. But how long will the quality cure take? Is it like an antibiotic or a prolonged rehabilitation?

No one knows the exact answer to this question. Among researchers, there is general agreement that about one-third of medical spending is not necessary. But there is no general agreement on how rapidly that excess can be eliminated. As Yogi Berra said, "Prediction is difficult, especially about the future."

Looking across the economy as a whole, there is no one path by which industries go from being less productive to more productive. It took decades before American automobile firms realized that they were nearly bankrupt and began to address their underlying problems. On the other hand, firms moved operations to the Internet at lightning speed, and e-commerce took off seemingly overnight. Health care change is unlikely to happen as rapidly as the Internet. But it needn't take decades either.

If the model for health care is the experience of other industries, let's start there. The best way to gauge how well an indus-

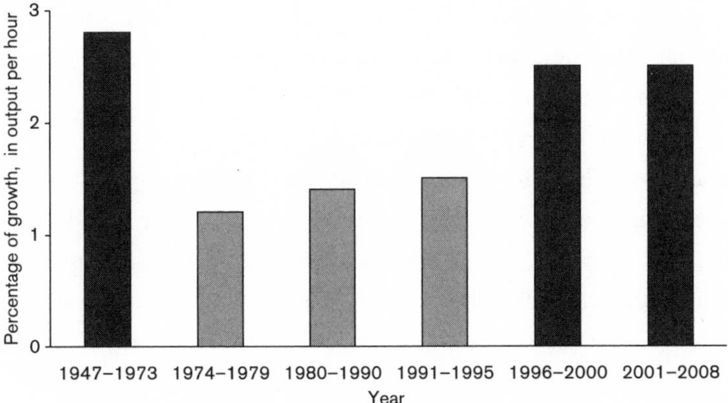

Figure 29. Productivity growth in the United States, 1947–2008. Graph shows the growth in output per hour in U.S. industry, according to data from the Bureau of Economic Analysis, www.bea.gov.

try is doing is by considering productivity growth. Productivity is output per input. When productivity rises, workers are able to produce more goods with fewer materials. This means that consumers can buy goods less expensively (input costs have fallen, and so can prices), and workers can be paid more (they do more in their time at work). Living standards in the economy as a whole increase proportionately to productivity.

Figure 29 shows productivity growth in the United States in the past half-century. From the period just after World War II until the early 1970s, productivity growth was rapid. On average, productivity grew nearly 3 percent annually. This was a "golden age" of U.S. prosperity; we look back fondly at those years. Starting with increasing oil prices in the mid-1970s, there ensued a two-decade period of low productivity growth. Average productivity growth fell to about 1.5 percent. "Stagflation" and other maladies became routine. By the early 1990s, most economists thought the "new normal" for the economy was a sustained low rate of productivity growth.

In about the mid-1990s, however, productivity growth rebounded. The rate of productivity growth from 1995 through 2008 was about 2.5 percent annually, just below the rate in the early post–World War II era. Incomes rose again, although this era was marked by a highly unequal distribution of the gains: some people did very well, others less so. Still, jobs were plentiful, government budgets were in surplus, and income mobility seemed possible for many.

The industries that led to the recent productivity revolution are shown in figure 30. Durable goods—makers of automobiles, computers, and other physical goods—are at the top of the list. The information technology and operations revolutions discussed in the previous chapter explain a good deal of the turnaround in durable goods productivity. The information technology industry is second from the top. These are the people who make software and other information systems—no surprise there. But the list has some surprises. Agriculture has become very productive, as has retail trade—the business of selling things to people. In considering agriculture, don't imagine the family farm; the modern farm is highly mechanized, capital intensive, and quite invested in science. Similarly, retail trade is not the corner store; Wal-Mart is more typical.

Farther down on the list are the economic laggards. Mining was very unproductive over this time period, although that is largely because mineral prices are extremely volatile, and this period experienced a reduction in many mineral prices. Health care, education, and social services actually showed negative reported productivity growth; by official data, health care is

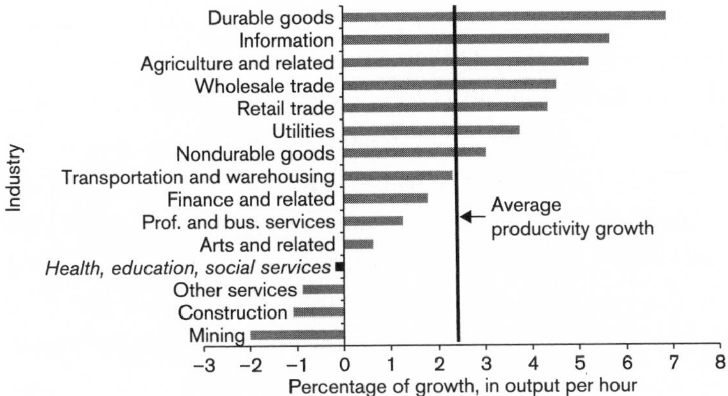

Figure 30. Productivity growth by industry, 1995–2005. Data are from Stephen D. Oliner, Daniel E. Sichel, and Kevin J. Stiroh, "Explaining a Productive Decade," *Brookings Papers on Economic Activity* 1 (2007): 81–152, table 5, www.brookings.edu/~/media/Projects/BPEA/Spring%202007/2007a_bpea_oliner.PDF.

doing less with more over time. This measure of productivity is understated, because quality is not adequately accounted for.[1] The official productivity estimate for health care is based on whether the price of specific services has increased or decreased over time (e.g., a hospital day), without accounting for whether the hospital day is more or less intensive, or higher or lower quality than it used to be. Still, the general sense that medical costs have been increasing without entirely realizing the expected benefits is right. The arts are another industry with low productivity growth.

One way to differentiate the leading industries from the laggards is by the use of information technology. To a first approximation, all industries with rapid productivity growth use IT extensively. Conversely, industries at the bottom of the list frequently lacked sustained use of information technology.

This impression is confirmed by more detailed analysis. Economists Stephen Oliner, Daniel Sichel, and Kevin Stiroh studied the sources of the increase in productivity growth over the past two decades. They related productivity growth at the industry level to a host of factors, including use of information technology. They found that higher IT use was associated with much more rapid growth in productivity. Industries that used IT above the median level grew 1.5 to 2.0 percentage points more rapidly than industries that were low users of information technology. Here, then, is our first metric: as we move health care from an economic laggard to a leading industry, growth might increase by 1.5 to 2.0 percentage points annually.

Another way to gauge the potential in health care is to look at what needs to be done and estimate how rapidly it can occur. Some of the health care problems we have noted are relatively straightforward, while others are much more difficult. Figure 31 presents guesses about how long different interventions would take to be implemented. The easiest changes are in the site of care. This involves people who are being hospitalized in expensive institutions when they could be treated just as well in less expensive ones or even on an outpatient basis. Knowing whether a patient needs intensive care is fairly easy. The groundwork to affect these transitions could be laid within one to two years, as provider systems hire necessary personnel, configure their electronic records to be alert to such patients, and orient their nurses and physicians to more appropriate settings.

Somewhat more difficult are changes that need to occur within institutions, to streamline the pathway of care for patients with various conditions. We have seen these changes too: rationalizing who receives stents and who does not, implementing care pathways for routine labor and delivery, and treating simple cases of

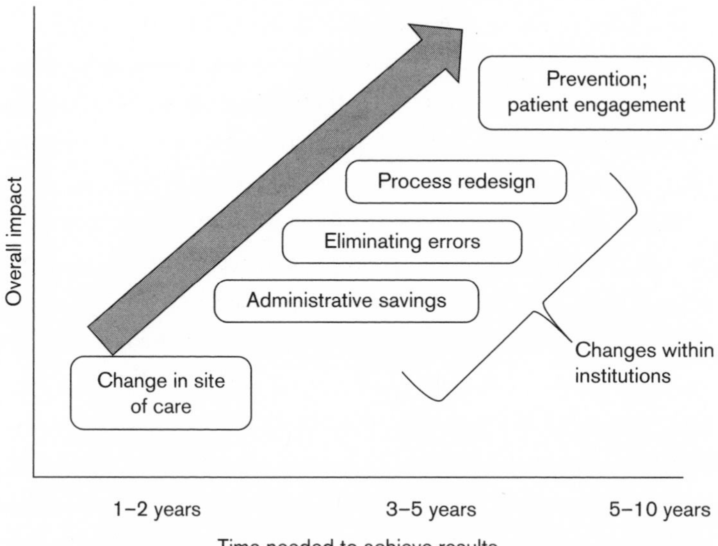

Figure 31. How long does it take to save one-third? Some reforms can take place rapidly, while others will need more time. Changing the site of care from expensive institutions to less expensive ones is most amenable to rapid intervention. Changes within institutions will take longer, and real patient engagement will likely be slowest.

lower back pain without sophisticated imaging or orthopedic consults. It will likely take some time for institutions to adopt these changes. My guess is that three to five years of work are required before major savings from these pathways can be realized.

The third tier of savings comes from populationwide prevention and patient engagement. Patients who do not take their medications will need to be counseled and encouraged to do so. Electronic interchange between physicians and patients will replace many face-to-face meetings. Decision-support software can be used to incorporate patient preferences into treatment plans. This set of changes is difficult. More experimentation is needed on how to interface with each set of patients and structure interventions in the way that makes most sense. Such experimentation will need at least five years to start bearing fruit and likely a decade before major savings can be realized.

Assuming that most of these changes can be implemented in the next decade, we would then experience a number of years when cost increases would decline—perhaps another five to ten years. All told, therefore, improving health care quality is a fifteen- to twenty-year venture. If we are able to pull out 30 percent of costs in fifteen years, this implies a cost reduction of 2 percent annually. If the transition takes twenty years, the implication is an average rate of cost savings of 1.5 percent annually. Here is the second piece of evidence: health care reform will increase productivity by perhaps 1.5 to 2 percent annually for fifteen to twenty years.

Higher productivity does not always mean spending reductions. As flat-screen TVs became better and cheaper, people bought more of them. With prices so low, why not add to the collection? Because the quantity of TV sets rose with falling prices, spending did not decline with productivity growth.

In the case of health care, however, productivity improvements are likely to show up primarily as spending reductions. We are already treating most people who are sick; we are just treating them poorly. Thus productivity improvements in health care will almost certainly come as lower spending growth.

• • •

Historically, the growth rate of medical spending has exceeded the growth rate of the economy as a whole by 1.5 to 2.0 percentage points annually. The gap was bigger in the 1960s—1980s and

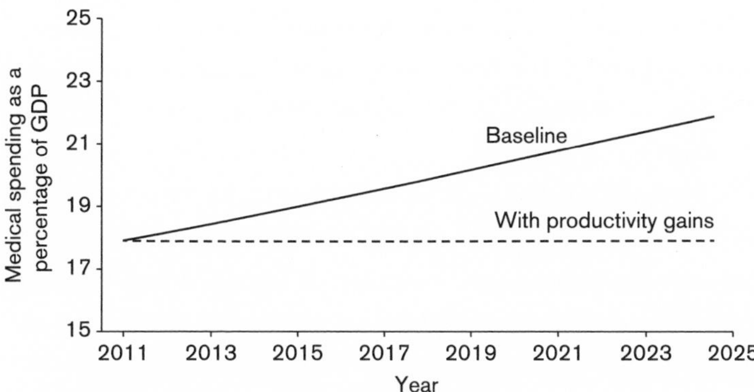

Figure 32. Trend in medical spending with and without productivity improvement. Medical spending projections are from the Centers for Medicare and Medicaid Services, *National Health Expenditure Accounts* (2013), www.cms.gov/Research-Statistics-Data-and-Systems/Statistics-Trends-and-Reports/NationalHealthExpendData/NationalHealthAccountsProjected.html.

then declined somewhat in the 1990s and 2000s. If the impact of health care reform is to reduce the growth of spending by 1.5 to 2.6 percentage points annually, that would essentially stabilize medical care as a share of the economy. Thus my expectation is that meaningful changes in the health system could lead to health care remaining constant as a share of the national economy for the next two decades or so. Figure 32 shows how this would affect medical care as a share of GDP, starting with the official estimates in 2011 and continuing from there.

A transformation of this magnitude would have a profound effect on the economy. On average, household income increases with overall economic growth. If the economy is 10 percent bigger, the average family will earn about 10 percent more. With less going into health benefits, more would be left for wages and salaries. Thus households would see much more rapid growth in their paychecks. For businesses, health insurance costs would increase on average no more rapidly than total sales.

The impact will likely be most profound for governments. Government revenue grows at roughly the rate of the economy. With a constant tax rate, the government gets more revenue only as national income increases. When increases in health costs exceed the growth of the economy, governments necessarily cut back on other services. In Massachusetts, for example, there has been a clear trade-off between health care and other goods and services in the past decade (figure 33): health care has taken more money, and everything else has suffered. If health costs are stabilized as a share of the economy, government spending on other goods and services can increase without taking more from taxpayers.

Massachusetts built on this observation in its recent health care cost initiative. Sensing that its commitment to universal coverage was in danger if it did not find a way to reduce the growth of medical spending—there is only so much that can be cut from other parts of government—Massachusetts passed legislation in the summer of 2012 that moves the health system away from fee-for-service payments, provides better information for consumers about the cost and quality of care, streamlines costly administrative processes, and encourages disclosure, apology, and early settlement offers in cases of adverse medical outcomes. On top of this, the state set a target for the growth of overall medical spending. Between 2014 and 2017, the growth rate of medical spending in the state is to equal the growth of the state economy.[2] From 2018 through 2022, the target growth rate is the growth of the economy less 0.5 percentage point. In 2023 and beyond, the target growth rate returns to the growth of the

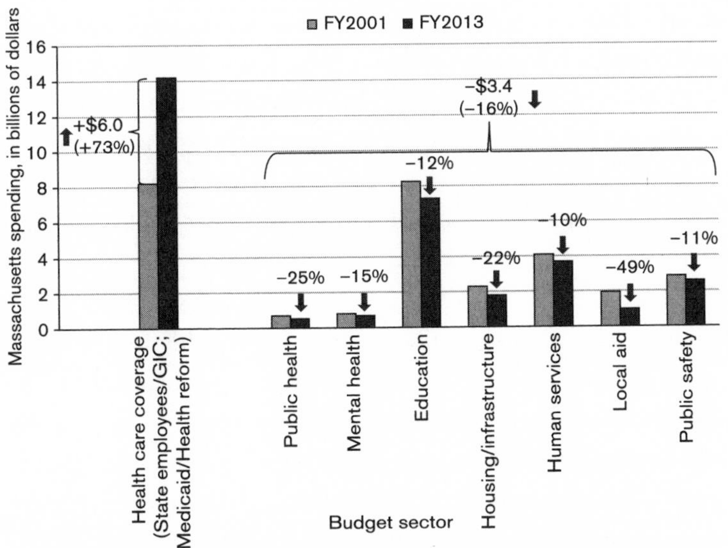

Figure 33. Health care and the Massachusetts state budget, 2001 and 2013. As spending on health care has increased, spending in other areas of government has declined. Spending in 2001 is adjusted to 2013 dollars by maintaining the same share of the economy. Data are from the Massachusetts Budget Browser, http://massbudget.org/browser/index.php. A similar chart for different years was published by the Blue Cross Blue Shield Foundation of Massachusetts, *Health Care Costs and Spending in Massachusetts: A Review of the Evidence* (Boston, MA: Blue Cross Blue Shield Foundation, 2012), http://bluecrossmafoundation.org/sites/default/files/Cost%20Deck%20March%20report.pdf.

economy. The actual sanctions for exceeding the target are not severe: a Health Policy Commission reviews the reasons why the target is not being met and requires payers and providers contributing to the excess to submit plans for returning to the target. Rather than threatening severe actions, the idea behind the target was to be very specific with the providers in the state about what constitutes a successful pattern of spending reduction.

Early in its implementation, the legislation seems to be having the intended effect. Health care provider systems are rapidly reorganizing so as to meet the cost target, and many of the specific changes that have been discussed are being implemented.

• • •

Suppose we are successful in eliminating roughly one-third of medical spending in the next two decades. What happens to cost growth after that point? At one level, we needn't worry about this just now. Two decades is so far out that it is impossible to guess what the medical system will be like. But there is always value in planning for the future. With that in mind, let me illustrate the possibilities.

Economists are of two minds about this question. The first group of economists expects cost growth to resume at its historic rate after waste has been eliminated. Underlying the long-term trend in medical spending is the development and diffusion of new ways of treating patients. This will continue—indeed, it should continue—and it will add to spending. A fair amount of research has gone into estimating the magnitude of this long-term component. Generally, economists believe that the technological component to medical cost increases is about 1 percent per year.[3] Thus this line of reasoning suggests that medical spending increases will return to the rate of economic growth plus 1 percent.

The second group of economists believes that cost growth will remain lower than the historical norm. The idea underlying this view is that there are always more productivity improvements to be had, even after the excessive spending we can identify today has been reduced.[4] The hallmark of productive businesses is not just that workers in those firms are productive, but that productivity is always increasing. Wal-Mart, Toyota, and Amazon are all continuously innovating in ways that lower costs of production. Given how complex the health care production process is, one might expect the same in health care. Adherents of this view do not have an explicit spending forecast in mind, but a natural benchmark is that medical care could continue at the productivity growth rate of the most successful industries, perhaps staying constant or falling as a share of total spending.

Yogi Berra was correct about the difficulty in making predictions. No one knows for sure how near-term changes will play out, let alone their longer-term effects. But in the end, there is certainly reason for optimism. If we do things right, the future of health care could be very bright indeed.

NOTES

1. COST, ACCESS, AND QUALITY

1. The statistics in this paragraph and the next two are from Robert J. Blendon, John M. Benson, and Kathleen J. Weldon, *The Medical System and the Uninsured,* Health Priorities Survey Report (Robert Wood Johnson Foundation, 2009). In 2009, costs were mentioned by 54 percent of respondents, insurance by 35 percent, accessibility by 16 percent, and poor quality by 13 percent.

2. Henry J. Aaron and Stuart M. Butler, "Four Steps to Better Health Care," *Washington Post,* July 6, 2003.

3. "Remarks by the President to a Joint Session of Congress on Health Care," Sept. 9, 2009, www.whitehouse.gov/the_press_office/Remarks-by-the-President-to-a-Joint-Session-of-Congress-on-Health-Care.

4. *3–27–10 Senate GOP Leader Mitch McConnell Delivers Weekly GOP Address on Health Care,* YouTube, Mar. 2010; "McConnell on Health Bill: 'We Can Do Better,'" *CNN,* Mar. 27, 2010.

5. Carmen DeNavas-Walt, Bernadette D. Proctor, and Jessica C. Smith, *Income, Poverty, and Health Insurance Coverage in the United States: 2010* (Washington, DC: U.S. Census Bureau, 2011).

6. Sara R. Collins, Michelle M. Doty, Ruth Robertson, and Tracy Garber, *Help on the Horizon: How the Recession Has Left Millions of Workers without Health Insurance, and How Health Reform Will Bring Relief—Findings from the Commonwealth Fund Biennial Health Insurance Survey of 2010* (Commonwealth Fund, 2011). See also tabulations from the Medical Expenditure Panel Survey: http://meps.ahrq.gov/mepsweb/data_files/publications/st336/stat336.pdf; and the Survey of Income and Program Participation: www.census.gov/prod/2006pubs/p70–106.pdf.

7. P.F. Adams, W.K. Kirzinger, and M.E. Martinez, "Summary Health Statistics for the U.S. Population: National Health Interview Survey, 2011," National Center for Health Statistics, *Vital and Health Statistics* 10, no. 255 (2012). In this survey, 43 percent of respondents indicate a reason directly related to cost.

8. Kaiser Family Foundation and Health Research and Educational Trust, *Employer Health Benefits: 2012 Annual Survey* (Kaiser Family Foundation, 2012).

9. Blendon, Benson, and Weldon, *The Medical System and the Uninsured.*

10. Institute of Medicine, *Insuring America's Health: Principles and Recommendations* (Washington, DC: National Academies Press, 2004).

11. *A Qualitative Analysis of the Heritage Foundation and Paul Group Proposals to Restructure the Health Insurance System* (Washington, DC: Congressional Budget Office, 1994).

12. "Session Laws," *Acts, 2006, Chapter 58: An Act Providing Access to Affordable, Quality, Accountable Health Care,* General Court, Apr. 2006.

13. Kaiser Commission on Medicaid and the Uninsured, *Medicaid Eligibility, Enrollment Simplification, and Coordination under the Affordable Care Act: A Summary of CMS's August 17, 2011 Proposed Rule and Key Issues to Consider* (Henry J. Kaiser Family Foundation, 2011), table 1: Medicaid Eligibility Categories under the Proposed Rule. Recent immigrants who are not eligible for Medicaid would be covered through the exchanges, where they would pay 2 percent of their income for insurance.

14. *CBO's Analysis of the Major Health Care Legislation Enacted in March 2010, before the Subcommittee on Health, Committee on Energy and Commerce, U.S. House of Representatives* (2011) (testimony of Douglas W. Elmendorf, Director).

15. Henry J. Kaiser Family Foundation, *Summary of New Health Reform Law,* issue brief, updated April 2013, http://kff.org/health-reform/fact-sheet/summary-of-new-health-reform-law/.

16. Congressional Budget Office, Letter to the Honorable Nancy Pelosi, March 20, 2010, table 4.

17. There are also other issues of concern. For example, some have worried about an implicit tax rate associated with the phase-out of the subsidies. Since my focus is primarily medical costs, I do not address this issue.

18. Carmen DeNavas-Walt, Bernadette D. Proctor, and Jessica C. Smith, *Income, Poverty, and Health Insurance Coverage in the United States: 2010* (Washington, DC: U.S. Census Bureau, 2011), table A2.

19. It is estimated that federal spending will be $4.1 trillion in 2016. See *The Economic and Budget Outlook: Fiscal Years 2012–2022* (Washington, DC: Congressional Budget Office, 2012).

20. Peter J. Cunningham, *State Variation in Primary Care Physician Supply: Implications for Health Reform Medicaid Expansions,* issue brief no. 19 (Center for Studying Health System Change, 2011).

21. *The Long-Term Outlook for Health Care Spending* (Washington, DC: Congressional Budget Office, 2007), table 3: Excess Cost Growth in Medicare, Medicaid, and All Other Spending on Health Care.

22. The ACA permits variation by age, geography, smoking status, and some health behaviors.

23. This includes New York, Massachusetts, New Jersey, and others. Jeffrey Clemens, "Regulatory Redistribution in the Market for Health Insurance," *Social Science Research Network,* Sept. 6, 2012, http://ssrn.com/abstract=2033424 or http://dx.doi.org/10.2139/ssrn.2033424.

24. David M. Cutler and Sarah J. Reber, "Paying for Health Insurance: The Tradeoff between Competition and Adverse Selection," *Quarterly Journal of Economics* 113, no. 2 (1998).

25. *Department of Health and Human Services, et al., Petitioners v. State of Florida, et al.,* Supreme Court of the United States, no. 11–398.

26. *National Health Expenditure Data* (Centers for Medicaid and Medicare Services, 2010), table 1. The same source is for the next paragraph.

27. *The Long-Term Outlook for Health Care Spending* (Washington, DC: Congressional Budget Office, 2007), table 3: Excess Cost Growth in Medicare, Medicaid, and All Other Spending on Health Care.

28. Lawrence H. Summers, "Some Simple Economics of Mandated Benefits," *American Economic Review* 79, no. 2 (1989): 177–83; and Jonathan Gruber, "The Incidence of Mandated Maternity Benefits," *American Economic Review* 84, no. 3 (1994): 622–41.

2. THE VALUE PROPOSITION

1. "Six Prescriptions for Health Care Change," *Consumer Reports*, March 2008, www.consumerreports.org/cro/2012/12/six-prescriptions-for-health-care-change/index.htm.

2. Some of this information comes from David Cutler, *Your Money or Your Life* (New York: Oxford University Press, 2004).

3. *The Cost of Prematurity to U.S. Employers*, issue brief (March of Dimes Foundation, 2008).

4. George S. Tolley, Donald Scott Kenkel, and Robert G. Fabian, *Valuing Health for Policy: An Economic Approach* (Chicago: University of Chicago, 1994); W. Kip Viscusi, "The Value of Risks to Life and Health," *Journal of Economic Literature* 31, no. 4 (1993): 1912–46; and Kevin M. Murphy and Robert H. Topel, "The Value of Health and Longevity," *Journal of Political Economy* 114, no. 5 (2006): 871–904.

5. *Kaiser Health Tracking Poll: Public Opinion on Health Care Issues* (Henry J. Kaiser Family Foundation, 2011).

6. David M. Cutler, "Equality, Efficiency, and Market Fundamentals: The Dynamics of International Medical Care Reform," *Journal of Economic Literature* (Sept. 2002): 881–906.

7. Pierre L. Yong, Robert S. Saunders, and LeighAnne Olsen, eds., *The Healthcare Imperative: Lowering Costs and Improving Outcomes*, Institute of Medicine Roundtable on Evidence-Based Medicine (Washington, DC: National Academies Press, 2010). The IOM revisited the issue, with similar results, in *Best Care at Lower Cost: The Path to Continuously Learning Health Care in America* (Washington, DC: National Academies Press, 2012); Donald M. Berwick and Andrew D. Hackbarth, "Eliminating Waste in U.S. Health Care," *Journal of the American*

Medical Association (2012), E1–E4; Jules Delaune and Wendy Everett, *Waste and Inefficiency in the U.S. Health Care System: Clinical Care: A Comprehensive Analysis in Support of System-wide Improvements* (New England Healthcare Institute, 2008).

8. Tarek M. Khalil, *Ergonomics in Back Pain: A Guide to Prevention and Rehabilitation* (New York: Van Nostrand Reinhold, 1993); Gunnar B.J. Andersson, "The Epidemiology of Spinal Disorders," in *The Adult Spine: Principles and Practice,* 2d ed. (Philadelphia: Lippincott-Raven, 1997), 93–141; and J. W. Frymoyer and William L. Cats-Baril, "An Overview of the Incidences and Costs of Low Back Pain," *Orthopedic Clinics of North America* 22, no. 2 (1991): 263–71.

9. Brook I. Martin, Richard A. Deyo, Sohail K. Mirza, et al., "Expenditures and Health Status among Adults with Back and Neck Problems," *Journal of the American Medical Association* 299, no. 6 (2008): 656–64.

10. Charles Kennedy, *Transforming Healthcare: Virginia Mason Medical Center's Pursuit of the Perfect Patient Experience* (Portland, OR: Productivity, 2010); Richard A. Deyo and Sohail K. Mirza, "The Case for Restraint in Spinal Surgery: Does Quality Management Have a Role to Play?" *European Spine Journal,* 18, no. 3 (2009): 331–37.

11. Richard A. Deyo and Sohail K. Mirza, "The Case for Restraint in Spinal Surgery: Does Quality Management Have a Role to Play?" *European Spine Journal* 18, no. 3 (2009): 331–37.

12. Jon D. Lurie, Nancy J. Birkmeyer, and James N. Weinstein, "Rates of Advanced Spinal Imaging and Spine Surgery," *Spine* 28, no. 6 (2003): 610–20.

13. Ibid.

14. ACOG Committee on Practice Bulletins—Obstetrics, "ACOG Practice Bulletin No. 107: Induction of Labor," *Obstetrics & Gynecology* 114, no. 2 (2009): 1:386–97.

15. *Maternal and Neonatal Outcomes of Elective Induction of Labor: A Systematic Review and Cost-Effectiveness Analysis* (2008), cited in *Elective Induction of Labor: Safety and Harms,* rep. no. 10-EHC004–3 (Agency for Health Care Research and Quality, 2009); Stacy T. Seyb et al., "Risk of Cesarean Delivery with Elective Induction of Labor at Term in Nulliparous Women," *Obstetrics & Gynecology* 94, no. 4 (1999): 600–607.

16. This estimate is from the 2010 Leapfrog Hospital Survey, cited in "Newborn Deliveries Are Scheduled Too Early, According to Hospital Watchdog Group," Leapfrog Group, Jan. 26, 2011, www.leapfroggroup.org/news/leapfrog_news/4788210. Other estimates can be found at Laura Landro, "A Push for More Pregnancies to Last 39 Weeks," *Wall Street Journal,* Mar. 1, 2011; and Steven L. Clark et al., "Neonatal and Maternal Outcomes Associated with Elective Term Delivery," *American Journal of Obstetrics and Gynecology* 200, no. 2 (2009): 156.e1–56.e4.

17. Wayne Rosamond et al., "Heart Disease and Stroke Statistics—2007 Update: A Report from the American Heart Association Statistics Committee and Stroke Statistics Subcommittee," *Circulation* 115 (2007): e69–e171, note 7.

18. Denise L. Campbell-Scherer and Lee A. Green, "ACC/AHA Guideline Update for the Management of ST-Segment Elevation Myocardial Infarction," *American Family Physician* 79, no. 12 (2009): 1080–86.

19. Ellen C. Keeley, Judith A. Boura, and Cindy L. Grines, "Primary Angioplasty versus Intravenous Thrombolytic Therapy for Acute Myocardial Infarction: A Quantitative Review of 23 Randomized Trials," *Lancet* 361, no. 9351 (2003): 13–20.

20. Judith S. Hochman et al., "Coronary Intervention for Persistent Occlusion after Myocardial Infarction," *New England Journal of Medicine* 355, no. 23 (2006): 2395–2407; and William E. Boden et al., "Optimal Medical Therapy with or without PCI for Stable Coronary Disease," *New England Journal of Medicine,* 356, no. 15 (2007): 1503–16.

21. William S. Weintraub et al., "Effect of PCI on Quality of Life in Patients with Stable Coronary Disease," *New England Journal of Medicine* 359, no. 7 (2008): 677–87.

22. D.N. Feldman et al. "Comparison of Outcomes of Percutaneous Coronary Interventions in Patients of Three Age Groups (<60, 60 to 80, and >80 years) (from the New York State Angioplasty Registry)," *American Journal of Cardiology* 98 (2006): 1334–39, note 7.

23. W.J. Martone et al., "Incidence and Nature of Endemic and Epidemic Nosocomial Infections," in J.V. Bennett and P.S. Brachman, eds., *Hospital Infections* (Boston: Little, Brown, 1992), 577–96, cited in R. Douglas Scott II, *The Direct Medical Costs of Healthcare-Associated Infections in U.S.*

Hospitals and the Benefits of Prevention (Atlanta: Centers for Disease Control, 2009); Association of Schools of Public Health, "Estimating Health Care-Associated Infections and Deaths in U.S. Hospitals, 2002," *Public Health Reports* 122 (2007): 160–66; Yong, Sanders, and Olson, *The Healthcare Imperative;* Ashish K. Jha et al., "Improving Safety and Eliminating Redundant Tests: Cutting Costs in U.S. Hospitals," *Health Affairs* 28, no. 5 (2009): 1475–84; and Martone et al., "Incidence and Nature," cited in Scott, *The Direct Medical Costs of Healthcare-Associated Infections.*

24. "Central Line-Associated Bloodstream Infection (CLABSI)," California Department of Public Health, www.cdph.ca.gov/programs/hai/Pages/CentralLine-associatedBloodStreamInfection(CLABSI).aspx.

25. Association for Professionals in Infection Control and Epidemiology, (APIC), *Guide to the Elimination of Catheter-Related Bloodstream Infections* (Becton, Dickinson, 2009).

26. Peter Pronovost et al., "An Intervention to Decrease Catheter-Related Bloodstream Infections in the ICU," *New England Journal of Medicine* 255, no. 26 (2006): 2725–32.

27. Patricia W. Stone, "Economic Burden of Healthcare-Associated Infections: An American Perspective," *Expert Review of Pharmacoeconomics & Outcomes Research* 9, no. 5 (2009): 417–22; and Scott, *The Direct Medical Costs of Healthcare-Associated Infections.*

28. "Aircraft Accident Rate Is Lowest in History," press release, International Air Transport Association, Feb. 23, 2011.

29. Malcolm Gladwell, "The Ethnic Theory of Plane Crashes," in *Outliers: The Story of Success* (New York: Little, Brown, 2008); see also Ori Brafman and Rom Brafman, *Sway: The Irresistible Pull of Irrational Behavior* (New York: Broadway Books, 2009), which describes an airplane crash involving Royal Dutch Airlines (KLM) and Pan Am that demonstrates similar themes.

30. Eric Malnic, "Korean Air Admits Crew Made Mistakes in Guam Crash," *Los Angeles Times,* Mar. 26, 1998.

31. Matthew L. Wald, "Crew of Airliner Received Warning Just before Guam Crash," *New York Times,* Mar. 24, 1998.

32. Shobha Phansalkar et al., "A Review of Human Factors Principles for the Design and Implementation of Medication Safety Alerts

in Clinical Information Systems," *Journal of the American Medical Informatics Association* 17, no. 5 (2010): 493–501.

33. All the statistics in this paragraph are from Stephen F. Jencks, Mark V. Williams, and Eric A. Coleman, "Rehospitalizations among Patients in the Medicare Fee-for-Service Program," *New England Journal of Medicine* 361, no. 3 (2009): 311–12.

34. Yong, Saunders, and Olsen, eds., *The Healthcare Imperative.*

35. Estimates by Richard J. Gilfillan in ibid.; Glenn M. Hackbarth, *Reforming America's Health Care Delivery System: Statement before the Senate Finance Committee Roundtable on Reforming America's Health Care Delivery System* (Medicare Payment Advisory Commission, 2009).

36. Yong, Saunders, and Olsen, eds., *The Healthcare Imperative,* 25 (Thomas J. Flottemesch); and Dana P. Goldman et al., "The Value of Elderly Disease Prevention," *Forum for Health Economics & Policy* 9, no. 2 (2006): 1–27.

37. David M. Cutler and Dan Ly, "The (Paper)Work of Medicine: Understanding International Medical Costs," *Journal of Economic Perspectives* 25, no. 2 (2011): 3–25.

38. David Cutler, Elizabeth Wikler, and Peter Basch, "Reducing Administrative Costs and Improving the Health Care System," *New England Journal of Medicine* 367 (2012): 1875–78; and Ezekiel Emanuel et al., "A Systemic Approach to Containing Health Care Spending," *New England Journal of Medicine* 367 (2012): 949–54.

39. Yong, Saunders, and Olsen, eds., *The Healthcare Imperative;* and James G. Kahn et al., "The Cost of Health Insurance Administration in California: Estimates for Insurers, Physicians, and Hospitals," *Health Affairs* 24, no. 6 (2005): 1629–39.

40. This analysis is drawn primarily from Employers Action Coalition on Healthcare Steering Committee, *Analysis of Administrative Simplification* (2003); and Mark Merlis, *Simplifying Administration of Health Insurance* (Washington, DC: National Academy of Public Administration/National Academy of Social Insurance, 2009). See also *Administrative Simplification for Medical Group Practices* (Medical Group Management Association, 2005).

41. Nick A. LeCuyer and Shubham Singhal, "Overhauling the US Health Care Payment System," *McKinsey Quarterly* (2007), 1–11.

42. Though these findings are not without controversy: *Examination of Health Care Cost Trends and Cost Drivers: Report for Annual Public Hearing*, Office of Attorney General Martha Coakley, Mar. 16, 2010; Paul Dreyer, "Executive Summary," *Analysis of the Attorney General's Report Titled "Examination of Health Care Cost Trends and Cost Drivers"* (Partners HealthCare, 2011); and Thomas O'Brien, Letter to Brent Henry, Vice President and General Counsel, Partners HealthCare System, Inc., June 25, 2010, Commonwealth of Massachusetts Office of the Attorney General.

43. *Testimony before the Committee on the Budget, United States Senate Cong.*, 1 (2012) (testimony of David M. Cutler, Otto Eckstein Professor of Applied Economics, Harvard University); and Yong, Saunders, and Olsen, eds., *The Healthcare Imperative.*

44. *Efforts to Combat Health Care Fraud and Abuse, Testimony before the Committee on Appropriations, Subcommittee on Labor, Health and Human Services, Education, and Related Agencies, U.S. House of Representatives Cong.* (2010) (testimony of William Corr, Deputy Secretary, Department of Health and Human Services).

45. *Report to the Congress: Regional Variation in Medicare Service Use* (Washington, DC: Medicare Payment Advisory Commission, 2011).

46. "Office Manager for Miami Home Health Company Sentenced to 78 Months in Prison for Role in $25 Million Health Care Fraud Scheme," press release, U.S. Department of Justice, Office of Public Affairs, Jan. 5, 2012.

47. David M. Cutler and Kaushik Ghosh, "The Potential for Cost Savings through Bundled Episode Payments," *New England Journal of Medicine* 366 (2012): 1075–77.

48. Mark W. Stanton, "The High Concentration of U.S. Health Care Expenditures," Agency for Healthcare Research and Quality, www.ahrq.gov/research/findings/factsheets/costs/expriach/index.html.

3. THE COST CONTROL DEBATE

1. Philip Musgrove et al., *World Health Report 2000—Health Systems: Improving Performance* (Geneva: World Health Organization, 2000).

2. Physicians' Working Group for Single-Payer National Health Insurance, "Proposal of the Physicians' Working Group for Single-

Payer National Health Insurance," *Journal of the American Medical Association* 290 (2003): 798–805.

3. *Proposal of the Physicians' Working Group for Single-Payer National Health Insurance—Executive Summary* (Physicians for a National Health Program, 2003). The statistics in this paragraph and the data for figure 9 come from *Health at a Glance 2011: OECD Indicators* (Organisation for Economic Co-operation and Development, 2011).

4. *Prescription Drugs: Companies Typically Charge More in the United States Than in Canada,* rep. no. 92–110 (U.S. General Accounting Office/Government Accountability Office, 1992); and *Prescription Drugs: Companies Typically Charge More in the United States Than in the United Kingdom,* rep. no. 94–29 (U.S. General Accounting Office/Government Accountability Office, 1994).

5. *International Federation of Health Plans: 2010 Comparative Price Report—Medical and Hospital Fees by Country* (International Federation of Health Plans, 2010).

6. Patricia M. Danzon and M.F. Furukawa, "International Prices and Availability of Pharmaceuticals in 2005," *Health Affairs* 27, no. 1 (2008): 221–33.

7. David M. Cutler, "Equality, Efficiency, and Market Fundamentals: The Dynamics of International Medical Care Reform," *Journal of Economic Literature* 40, no. 3 (2002): 881–906.

8. *Annual Report, 2009/2010* (Toronto: Cardiac Care Network, 2010).

9. David M. Cutler, Robert S. Huckman, and Jonathan T. Kolstad, "Input Constraints and the Efficiency of Entry: Lessons from Cardiac Surgery," *American Economic Journal: Economic Policy* 2, no. 1 (2010): 51–76; and "Hospital Structural Measures—Cardiac Surgery Registry," Medicare, 2011, http://data.medicare.gov/dataset/Hospital-Structural-Measures-Cardiac-Surgery-Regis/easc-zwde.

10. D.T. Ko et al., "Temporal Trends in the Use of Percutaneous Coronary Intervention and Coronary Artery Bypass Surgery in New York State and Ontario," *Circulation* 121, no. 24 (2010): 2635–44.

11. *Health at a Glance 2011: OECD Indicators.*

12. The classic example is Canada in the early 1990s. See David Cutler, "Equality, Efficiency, and Market Fundamentals: The Dynam-

ics of International Medical Care Reform," *Journal of Economic Literature* (2002): 881–906.

13. Alessandra Lo Scalzo et al., *Health Care Systems in Transition: Italy* (European Observatory on Health Care Systems, 2001).

14. "Nurses Criticise Overseas Recruitment," *BBC News World Edition,* May 21, 2001; and Carol Propper and John Van Reenen, "Paying the Price," *Guardian,* Feb. 8, 2008.

15. "Medical Devices," FDA: U.S. Food and Drug Administration, Dec. 9, 2011.

16. Newt Gingrich, *Winning the Future: A 21st Century Contract with America* (Washington, DC: Regnery, 2005), 109.

17. Between 1960 and 2010, dental care costs increased from $64 per capita to $339 per capita (in 2010 dollars), for a 3.4 percent annual growth. Personal health care spending overall increased from $748 per capita to $7,081 per capita (in 2010 dollars), for 4.6 percent annual growth.

18. According to the American Pet Product Association, spending on veterinary care increased from $7.1 billion in 2001 to $13.4 billion in 2011, for a 4.2 percent real annual increase. This is slightly greater than the spending increase for human care over this time period.

19. Arnold S. Relman, "The Health of Nations," *New Republic,* Mar. 7, 2005.

20. Joseph P. Newhouse and the Insurance Experiment Group, *Free for All? Lessons from the RAND Health Insurance Experiment* (Cambridge, MA: Harvard University Press, 1996).

21. Melinda Beeuwkes Buntin et al., "Healthcare Spending and Preventive Care in High-Deductible and Consumer-Directed Health Plans," *American Journal of Managed Care* 17, no. 3 (2011): 222–30.

22. Willard G. Manning et al., "Health Insurance and the Demand for Medical Care: Evidence from a Randomized Experiment," *American Economic Review* 77, no. 3 (1987): 251–77; Kevin F. O'Grady, Willard G. Manning, Joseph P. Newhouse, and Robert H. Brook, "The Impact of Cost Sharing on Emergency Department Use," *New England Journal of Medicine* 314, no. 2 (1985): 122–23; and Richard E. Johnson, Michael J. Goodman, Mark C. Hornbrook, and Michael B. Eldredge, "The Effect of Increased Prescription Drug Cost-Sharing on Medical Care

Utilization and Expenses of Elderly Health Maintenance Organization Members," *Medical Care* 35, no. 11 (1997): 1119–31.

23. Amitabh Chandra, Jonathan Gruber, and Robin McKnight, "Patient Cost-Sharing, Hospitalization Offsets, and the Design of Optimal Health Insurance for the Elderly," *American Economic Review* 100, no. 1 (2010): 193–213.

24. Dana P. Goldman, Geoffrey F. Joyce, and Yuhui Zheng, "Prescription Drug Cost Sharing: Associations with Medication and Medical Utilization and Spending and Health," *Journal of the American Medical Association* 298, no. 1 (2007): 61–69.

25. "Medicare," Romney for President, Sept. 2012, www.mittromney.com/issues/medicare.

26. "Medicare on Main Street—More Endorsements for Premium Support to Save Medicare," www.gop.gov/policy-news/12/10/19/medicare-on-main-street.

4. THE QUALITY CURE

1. Douglas McCarthy, Kimberly Mueller, and Jennifer Wrenn, *Kaiser Permanente: Bridging the Quality Divide with Integrated Practice, Group Accountability, and Health Information Technology* (Commonwealth Fund, 2009); "A Focus on KP HealthConnect," *Permanente Journal* (2004), 1–40; Anna-Lisa Silvestre, Valerie M. Sue, and Jill Y. Allen, "If You Build It, Will They Come? The Kaiser Permanente Model of Online Health Care," *Health Affairs* 28, no. 2 (2009): 334–44; "Kaiser Permanente HealthConnect® Electronic Health Record," Kaiser Permanente News Center, http://xnet.kp.org/newscenter/aboutkp/healthconnect/index.html.

2. Jamie Ferguson, *Challenges and Learning in the New Era of Health IT* (Kaiser Permanente, 2010); Marianne K. McGee, "Microsoft, Kaiser Permanente Launch E-Health Record Pilot," *InformationWeek,* June 9, 2008; Marianne K. McGee, "Microsoft Unveils Free Web Health Tools for Consumers," *Information Week,* Oct. 4, 2007; and Lucien Wulsin and Adam Dougherty, *Health Information Technology-Electronic Health Records: A Primer* (California Research Bureau, 2008).

3. Adapted from "Kaiser Permanente HealthConnect® Electronic Health Record."

4. Catherine Chen et al., "The Kaiser Permanente Electronic Health Record: Transforming and Streamlining Modalities of Care," *Health Affairs* 28, no. 2 (2009): 323–33.

5. Yi Yvonne Zhou et al., "Improved Quality at Kaiser Permanente through E-mail between Physicians and Patients," *Health Affairs* 29, no. 7 (2010): 1370–75; and Louise L. Liang, *Connected for Health: Using Electronic Health Records to Transform Care Delivery* (San Francisco: Jossey-Bass, 2010).

6. Terhilda Garrido, "Making the Business Case for Hospital Information Systems—A Kaiser Permanente Investment Decision," *Journal of Health Care Finance* 31, no. 2 (2004): 16–25.

7. "What Health Systems Can Learn from Kaiser Permanente: An Interview with Hal Wolf," *McKinsey Quarterly* (July 2009).

8. "A Focus on KP HealthConnect," *Permanente Journal* (2004), 1–40.

9. Kaiser employs about 15,853 physicians ("About Kaiser Permanente: Fast Facts about Kaiser Permanente," Kaiser Permanente News Center, http://xnet.kp.org/newscenter/aboutkp/fastfacts.html). A savings of $500 million per year therefore means $31,540 in reduced costs per primary care physician. There are about 209,000 primary care doctors in the country ("Primary Care Workforce Facts and Stats No. 1: The Number of Practicing Primary Care Physicians in the United States," *Primary Care Workforce Facts and Stats No. 1* [Agency for Healthcare Research and Quality, 2011]), leading to the $6.6 billion estimate.

10. Douglas McCarthy, Kimberly Mueller, and Jennifer Wrenn, *Organized Health Care Delivery System—Kaiser Permanente: Bridging the Quality Divide with Integrated Practice, Group Accountability, and Health Information Technology* (Commonwealth Fund, 2009), www.commonwealthfund.org/~/media/Files/Publications/Case%20Study/2009/Jun/1278_McCarthy_Kaiser_case_study_624_update.pdf.

11. Douglas McCarthy, Kimberly Mueller, and Jennifer Wrenn, *Mayo Clinic: Multidisciplinary Teamwork, Physician-Led Governance, and Patient-Centered Culture Drive World-Class Health Care* (Commonwealth Fund, 2009).

12. William James Mayo, "The Necessity of Cooperation in Medicine," *Mayo Clinic Proceedings* 75 (2000): 553–56.

13. "U.S. News: Health," *U.S. News & World Report,* http://health.usnews.com/best-hospitals/area/mn/mayo-clinic-6611MAYO.

14. Unless otherwise noted, the facts and figure in this section come from Alfred S. Casale et al., "ProvenCare^{SM}: A Provider-Driven Pay-for-Performance Program for Acute Episodic Cardiac Surgical Care," *Annals of Surgery* 246, no. 4 (2007): 613–23; and Douglas McCarthy, Kimberly Mueller, and Jennifer Wrenn, *Geisinger Health System: Achieving the Potential of System Integration through Innovation, Leadership, Measurement, and Incentives* (Commonwealth Fund, 2009).

15. There are about 1,081 CABGs per million adults annually. Andrew J. Epstein et al., "Coronary Revascularization Trends in the United States," *Journal of the American Medical Association* 305, no. 17 (2011): 1769–76. Multiplied by the U.S. population, this yields about 250,000 CABGs annually. The cost of a CABG episode is estimated to be approximately $43,000; see David Cutler and Kaushik Ghosh, "The Potential for Cost Savings through Bundled Episode Payments," *New England Journal of Medicine* 366, no. 12 (2012): 1075–77. To estimate the savings from national adoption of the ProvenCare model, I assume savings of 5 percent on the inpatient share of the total, which is equal to about $35,000 per episode. This yields approximately $400 million annually.

16. Northern New England Perinatal Quality Improvement Network (NNEPQIN) and American Congress of Obstetricians and Gynecologists (ACOG), *Guideline Suggestions for Elective Labor Induction,* Jan. 20, 2012; Vincenzo Berghella, *Preterm Birth: Prevention and Management* (Chichester, West Sussex: Wiley-Blackwell, 2010).

17. "Hospitals Make Progress in Eliminating Early Elective Deliveries: Good News, but More Work Needs to Be Done," Leapfrog Group, Jan. 25, 2012, www.leapfroggroup.org/news/leapfrog_news/4827337.

18. *Days of Healing: Intermountain Healthcare Annual Report 2010* (Intermountain Healthcare, 2011).

19. For information on this intervention, see Bryan T. Oshiro et al., "Decreasing Elective Deliveries before 39 Weeks of Gestation in an Integrated Health Care System," *Obstetrics & Gynecology* 113, no. 4 (2009): 804–11.

20. Brent C. James and Lucy A. Savitz, "How Intermountain Trimmed Health Care Costs through Robust Quality Improvement Efforts," *Health Affairs* 30, no. 6 (2011): 1185–91.

21. Jeffrey G. Jarvik et al., "Rapid Magnetic Resonance Imaging vs. Radiographs for Patients with Low Back Pain: A Randomized Clinical Trial," *Journal of the American Medical Association* 289, no. 21 (2003): 2810–18, cited in C. Craig Blackmore, Robert S. Mecklenburg, and Gary S. Kaplan, "At Virginia Mason, Collaboration among Providers, Employers, and Health Plans to Transform Care Cut Costs and Improved Quality," *Health Affairs* 30, no. 9 (2011): 1680–87.

22. *Improving Quality, Lowering Costs: The Role of Health Care Delivery System Reform, Testimony before the Committee on Health, Education, Labor and Pensions,* U.S. Senate (2011) (testimony of Gary S. Kaplan).

23. Charles Kenney, *Transforming Health Care: Virginia Mason Medical Center's Pursuit of the Perfect Patient Experience* (Boca Raton: CRC, 2011).

24. "People & Places: Waking Up and Smelling the Coffee—Collaborating with Employers Led Virginia Mason to Cheaper Care," *Health Affairs* 30, no. 9 (2011): 1688.

25. Jarvik et al., "Rapid Magnetic Resonance Imaging vs. Radiographs," cited in Blackmore, Mecklenburg, and Kaplan, "At Virginia Mason, Collaboration among Providers, Employers, and Health Plans"; "Toyota Production System," Toyota Motor Company, www.toyota.com.au/toyota/company/operations/toyota-production-system.

26. Vanessa Fuhrmans, "A Novel Plan Helps Hospital Wean Itself Off Pricey Tests," *Wall Street Journal,* Jan. 12, 2007, cited in Timothy W. Flynn, Britt Smith, and Roger Chou, "Clinical Commentary: Appropriate Use of Diagnostic Imaging in Low Back Pain: A Reminder That Unnecessary Imaging May Do as Much Harm as Good," *Journal of Orthopaedic & Sports Physical Therapy,* 41, no. 11 (2011).

27. Robert S. Mecklenburg and Gary S. Kaplan, *2007 Annual Report: The Marketplace Collaborative Project* (Center for Health Care Solutions at Virginia Mason, 2008).

28. *Improving Quality, Lowering Costs* (testimony of Gary S. Kaplan).

29. Fuhrmans, "A Novel Plan," cited in Flynn, Smith, and Chou, "Clinical Commentary."

30. David M. Cutler, Karen Davis, and Kristof Stremikis, *The Impact of Health Reform on Health System Spending,* issue brief (Commonwealth Fund, May 2010).

31. Ellyn Boukus, Alwyn Cassil, and Ann S. O'Malley, *A Snapshot of U.S. Physicians: Key Findings from the 2008 Health Tracking Physician Survey,* rep. no. 35 (Center for Studying Health System Change, 2009).

32. Richard B. Freeman, "Wal-Mart Innovation and Productivity: A Viewpoint," *Canadian Journal of Economics* 44, no. 2 (2011): 486–508; Don Soderquist, *The Wal-Mart Way: The Inside Story of the Success of the World's Largest Company* (Nashville, TN: Thomas Nelson, 2005).

5. IT'S WHAT YOU KNOW

1. Dustin Charles, Michael Furukawa, and Meghan Hufstader, *Electronic Health Record Systems and Intent to Attest to Meaningful Use among Non-Federal Acute Care Hospitals in the United States: 2008–2011*, issue brief no. 1 (Office of the National Coordinator for Health Information Technology, 2012); and Catherine M. DesRoches et al., "Electronic Health Records in Ambulatory Care—A National Survey of Physicians," *New England Journal of Medicine* 359, no. 1 (2008): 50–60. See also David Blumenthal et al., *Health Information Technology in the United States: The Information Base for Progress* (Princeton, NJ: Robert Wood Johnson Foundation; 2006); *Key Capabilities of an Electronic Health Record system: Letter Report* (Washington, DC: Institute of Medicine, 2003).

2. James B. Conway and Saul N. Weingart, *Organizational Change in the Face of Highly Public Errors I. The Dana-Farber Cancer Institute Experience* (Washington, DC: Agency for Health Care Quality and Research, 2005); Scott Allen, "With Work, Dana-Farber Learns from '94 Mistakes," *Boston Globe,* Nov. 30, 2004; Christine Gorman, "The Disturbing Case of the Cure That Killed the Patient," *Time,* Apr. 3, 1995; and Mark Crane, "Who Caused This Tragic Medication Mistake," *Medical Economics* 19 (2001): 49.

3. Michael R. Cohen, ed., *Medication Errors,* 2d ed. (Washington, DC: American Pharmacists Association, 2007).

4. *Crossing the Quality Chasm: A New Health System for the 21st Century* (Washington, DC: National Academies, 2001); Joseph Antos et al.,

Bending the Curve: Effective Steps to Address Long-Term Health Care Spending Growth (Washington, DC: Brookings Institution, 2009); see also Newt Gingrich, Dana Pavey, and Anne Woodbury, *Saving Lives & Saving Money: Transforming Health and Healthcare,* (Washington, DC: Gingrich Communications, 2003); and Douglas Johnston et al., *The Value of Computerized Provider Order Entry in Ambulatory Settings,* Center for Information Technology Leadership, www.partners.org/cird /pdfs/CITL_ACPOE_Full.pdf; David W. Bates et al., "Effect of Computerized Physician Order Entry and a Team Intervention on Prevention of Serious Medication Errors" (abstract), *Journal of the American Medical Association* 280, no. 15 (1998): 1311–16; and Philip Aspden et al., *Preventing Medication Errors* (Washington, DC: National Academies, 2007).

5. Linda T. Kohn, Janet Corrigan, and Molla S. Donaldson, *To Err Is Human: Building a Safer Health System* (Washington, DC: National Academies, 2000).

6. For description of the data and results, see Chun-Hu Hsiao and Esther Hing, "Use and Characteristics of Electronic Health Record Systems among Office-Based Physician Practices: United States, 2001–2012," NCHS data brief no. 111, December 2012. Any EMR /EHR system refers to a yes response to the question "Does this practice use electronic medical records or electronic health records (not including billing records)?" The basic system is as described in table 8.

7. The Department of Commerce estimated that total capital expenditures by General Medical and Surgical Hospitals came to $55 billion in 2008 (2008 Annual Capital Expenditures Survey). Healthcare Information and Management Systems Society estimated that 17.76 percent of capital expense was for IT (2010 Annual Report of the U.S. Hospital Market). In 2007, there were 5.1 million employees in general medical and surgical hospitals (U.S. Census Bureau).

8. Francois M. Laflamme, Wayne E. Pietraszek, and Nilesh V. Rajadhyax, "McKinsey on Business Technology," *McKinsey Quarterly* 20 (2010): 1–33. They estimate a cost of about $100,000 per bed, which totals $20 million for a two-hundred-bed hospital.

9. General medical and surgical hospitals spent $55 billion on capital spending in 2008, and there were 5,100 such hospitals in

2007 (Census Bureau, www.census.gov/econ/aces/xls/2008/Full%20 Report.htm).

10. *Da Vinci Robot Investor Presentation: Q2 2012* (Intuitive Surgical, 2012); John Carreyrou, "Surgical Robot Examined in Injuries," *Wall Street Journal | Health,* May 4, 2010.

11. Nick A. LeCuyer and Shubham Singhal, "Overhauling the US Health Care Payment System," *McKinsey Quarterly* (2007): 1–11.

12. Congressional Budget Office, Letter to the Honorable Charles B. Rangel, Jan. 21, 2009.

13. "Radiation: Pros & Cons," Prostate Centre, www.prostatecan cercare.com/treatment/external_pc.html; Massoud Al-Abany et al., "Long-term Symptoms after External Beam Radiation Therapy for Prostate Cancer with Three or Four Fields," *Acta Oncologica* 41, no. 6 (2002): 532–42; and Mayo Clinic Staff, "External Beam Radiation for Prostate Cancer," Mayo Clinic, Feb. 26, 2011, www.mayoclinic.com /health/external-beam-radiation-for-prostate-cancer/MY01632.

14. Kaiser Family Foundation and Health Research and Educational Trust, *2011 Employer Health Benefits Survey* (Washington, DC: Henry J. Kaiser Family Foundation, 2011).

15. Benjamin J. Davison, Lesley F. Degner, and Timothy R. Morgan, "Information and Decision-Making Preferences of Men with Prostate Cancer," *Oncology Nursing Forum* 22, no. 9 (1995): 1401–8; Benjamin J. Davison and Erin N. Breckon, "Impact of Health Information-Seeking Behavior and Personal Factors on Preferred Role in Treatment Decision Making in Men with Newly Diagnosed Prostate Cancer," *Cancer Nursing* 35, no. 6 (2012): 411–18; and Ann B. Flood et al., "The Importance of Patient Preference in the Decision to Screen for Prostate Cancer," *Journal of General Internal Medicine* 11, no. 6 (1996): 342–49.

16. Benjamin D. Sommers et al., "Predictors of Patient Preferences and Treatment Choices for Localized Prostate Cancer," *Cancer* 113, no. 8 (2008): 2058–67.

17. Flood et al., "The Importance of Patient Preference"; and Erol Onel et al., "Assessment of the Feasibility and Impact of Shared Decision Making in Prostate Cancer," *Urology* 51 (1998): 63–66.

18. Floyd J. Fowler Jr. et al., "Comparison of Recommendations by Urologists and Radiation Oncologists for Treatment of Clinically

Localized Prostate Cancer," *Journal of the American Medical Association* 283, no. 24 (2000): 3217–22; Allison A. Chapple et al., "Is 'Watchful Waiting' a Real Choice for Men with Prostate Cancer? A Qualitative Study," *BJU International* 90, no. 3 (2002): 257–64; and Durado Brooks, "To Treat or Not to Treat Prostate Cancer: That Is the Question," American Cancer Society, Jan. 18, 2012, www.cancer.org/cancer/news/expertvoices/post/2012/01/18/to-treat-or-not-to-treat-prostate-cancer-that-is-the-question.aspx.

19. For more on this, see David Cutler, Elizabeth Wikler, and Peter Basch, "Reducing Administrative Costs and Improving the Health Care System," *New England Journal of Medicine* 367 (2012): 1875–78; and Elizabeth Wikler, Peter Basch, and David M. Cutler, *Paper Cuts: Reducing Health Care Administrative Costs* (Center for American Progress, 2012).

20. Richard Hillestad, Richard, James Bigelow, Anthony Bower, Federico Girosi, Robin Meili, Richard Scoville, and Roger Taylor, "Can Electronic Medical Record Systems Transform Health Care? Potential Health Benefits, Savings, and Costs," *Health Affairs* 24, no. 5 (Sept./Oct. 2005): 1103–17.

21. Arthur L. Kellermann and Spencer S. Jones, "What It Will Take to Achieve the As-Yet-Unfulfilled Promises of Health Information Technology," *Health Affairs* 32, no. 1 (2013): 63–68.

22. Ibid., 64.

23. Catherine M. DesRoches et al., "Small, Nonteaching, and Rural Hospitals Continue to Be Slow in Adopting Electronic Health Record Systems," *Health Affairs* 31, no. 5 (2012): 1092–99.

24. David M. Cutler, "The Next Wave of Corporate Medicine—How We All Might Benefit," *New England Journal of Medicine* 361, no. 6 (2009): 549–51.

25. *Examination of Health Care Cost Trends and Cost Drivers—Pursuant to G.L.C. 118G, ∬ 61/2(b): Report for Annual Public Hearing* (Office of Massachusetts Attorney General Martha Coakley, 2011).

26. Carey Goldberg, "A Behind-the-Ledger Look at Partners HealthCare's Billions," WBUR's CommonHealth, Aug. 2011, http://commonhealth.wbur.org/2011/08/partners-healthcare-billions; "Transparency on Reserves," Partners HealthCare, www.connectwithpartners

.org/2011/09/19/transparency-on-reserves/; and Kay Lazar, "Hospitals Report Hefty Reserves," *Boston Globe,* May 18, 2010.

27. John R. Hicks, "Annual Survey of Economic Theory: The Theory of Monopoly," *Econometrica* 3, no. 1 (1935).

6. PRICING THE PRICELESS

1. The title of this chapter is taken from Joseph Newhouse, *Pricing the Priceless: A Healthcare Conundrum* (Cambridge, MA: MIT Press, 2002).

2. Amy Finkelstein and Robin McKnight, "What Did Medicare Do? The Initial Impact of Medicare on Mortality and Out of Pocket Medical Spending," *Journal of Public Economics* 92 (2008): 1644–69.

3. Amy Finkelstein, "The Aggregate Effects of Health Insurance: Evidence from the Introduction of Medicare," *Quarterly Journal of Economics,* 122, no. 3 (2007): 1–37.

4. René J. Dubos, "The Diseases of Civilizations," *Milbank Memorial Fund Quarterly* 47 (1969): 327–29.

5. David Card, Carlos Dobkin, and Nicole Maestas, "Does Medicare Save Lives?" *Quarterly Journal of Economics* 124, no. 2 (2009): 597–636; and J. Michael McWilliams et al., "Health of Previously Uninsured Adults after Acquiring Medicare Coverage," *Journal of the American Medical Association* 298 (2007): 2886–94.

6. The figures in the paragraph are for Chicago but would be approximately the same anywhere.

7. "2011–2012 Physician Salary Survey," Profiles, Sept. 2011, www.profilesdatabase.com/resources/2011-2012-physician-salary-survey.

8. Anupam B. Jena et al., "Malpractice Risk according to Physician Specialty," *New England Journal of Medicine* 365, no. 7 (2011): 629–36.

9. The system is slightly more complicated, as there are outlier payments for people in the hospital a long time. I ignore this in the discussion.

10. Technology helped too; the most common reason for admission at the time was for cataract surgery, which became an outpatient procedure.

11. The figures in this paragraph are from U.S. Department of Health and Human Services, *Health United States, 2012.*

12. See David Draper et al., "Studying the Effects of the DRG-Based Prospective Payment System on Quality of Care: Design, Sampling, and Fieldwork," *Journal of the American Medical Association,* 264, no. 15 (1990): 1956–61.

13. Mireille Jacobson et al., "How Medicare's Payment Cuts for Cancer Chemotherapy Drugs Changed Patterns of Treatment," *Health Affairs* 29, no. 7 (2010): 1391–99.

14. Winnie C. Yip, "Physician Response to Medicare Fee Reductions: Changes in the Volume of Coronary Artery Bypass Graft (CABG) Surgeries in the Medicare and Private Sectors," *Journal of Health Economics* 17 (1998): 675–99.

15. *Factors Underlying the Growth in Medicare's Spending for Physicians' Services* (Washington, DC: Congressional Budget Office, 2007).

16. This discussion draws on Randall P. Ellis, and Thomas G. McGuire, "Provider Behavior under Prospective Reimbursement: Cost Sharing and Supply," *Journal of Health Economics* 5, no. 2 (June 1986): 129–51, and subsequent literature.

17. Francois De Brantes, Meredith B. Rosenthal, and Michael Painter, "Building a Bridge from Fragmentation to Accountability—The Prometheus Payment Model," *New England Journal of Medicine* 361, no. 11 (2009): 1033–36.

18. David M. Cutler and Kaushik Ghosh, "The Potential for Cost Savings through Bundled Episode Payments," *New England Journal of Medicine* 366 (2012): 1075–77.

19. *Dartmouth Atlas of Health Care* (Trustees of Dartmouth College, 2012).

20. High-spending areas are areas that are at or above the seventy-fifth percentile of costs. Low-spending areas are areas that are at or below the twenty-fifth percentile of costs.

21. Lyle Nelson, "Lessons from Medicare's Demonstration Projects on Value-Based Payment" (working paper, Congressional Budget Office, January 2012).

22. Jerry Cromwell, Debra A. Dayhoff, and Armen H. Thoumaian, "Cost Savings and Physician Responses to Global Bundled Payments for Medicare Heart Bypass Surgery," *Health Care Financing Review* 19, no. 1 (1997): 41–57; and Harriet L. Komisar, Judy Feder, and Paul B.

Ginsburg, *"Bundling" Payment for Episodes of Hospital Care: Issues and Recommendations for the New Pilot Program in Medicare* (Center for American Progress, 2011).

23. Armen H. Thoumaian, Linda M. Magno, and Cynthia K. Mason, "Medicare and Bundled Payments," in Pierre L. Yong, Robert S. Saunders, and LeighAnne Olsen, eds., *The Healthcare Imperative: Lowering Costs and Improving Outcomes,* Institute of Medicine Roundtable on Evidence-Based Medicine (Washington, DC: National Academies Press, 2010).

24. Sarah Kliff, "Health Reform at 2: Why American Health Care Will Never Be the Same," *Washington Post,* March 23, 2012.

25. "Bundled Payments for Care Improvement," Centers for Medicare & Medicaid Services, Sept. 6, 2012, www.innovations.cms.gov/initiatives/bundled-payments/index.html.

26. Josh Gray and Sarah Gabriel, "Select Results: 2011 Accountable Payment Survey," Advisory Board Company, 2012, www.advisory.com/Research/Financial-Leadership-Council/White-Papers/2012/Accountable-Payment-Survey.

27. Zirui Song et al., "Health Care Spending and Quality in Year 1 of the Alternative Quality Contract," *New England Journal of Medicine* 365 (2011): 909–18; and Zirui Song et al., "The 'Alternative Quality Contract,' Based on a Global Budget, Lowered Medical Spending and Improved Quality," *Health Affairs* 31, no. 8 (2012): 1–10.

28. Robert Weisman, "Partners Recasts Deal with Tufts, Limiting Pay," *Boston Globe,* Jan. 19, 2012.

29. U.S. Department of Health and Human Services, "More Doctors, Hospitals Partner to Coordinate Care for People with Medicare," news release, Jan. 10, 2013.

30. Pieter Van Herck et al., "Systematic Review: Effects, Design Choices, and Context of Pay-for-Performance in Health Care," *BMC Health Services Research* (2010): 10:247.

31. Ezekiel J. Emanuel, "The Arkansas Innovation," *New York Times,* Sept. 5, 2012.

32. Kaiser Family Foundation, *Emerging Medicaid Accountable Care Organizations: The Role of Managed Care* (Washington, DC: Kaiser Family Foundation, 2012).

33. Blue Cross Blue Shield Foundation, *Summary of Chapter 224 of the Acts of 2012* (Boston, MA: Blue Cross Blue Shield Foundation, 2012).

34. "People & Places—Capitation by Any Other Name: An Insurer Adds a New Twist to an Old Idea," *Health Affairs* 30, no. 1 (2011): 62.

7. TAKE ME TO YOUR LEADER

1. "Suzanne" is a pseudonym. The case is detailed in Benjamin P. Sachs, "A 38-Year-Old Woman with Fetal Loss and Hysterectomy," *Journal of the American Medical Association* 294, no. 7 (2005): 833–40.

2. George E. Cooper, Maurice D. White, and John K. Lauber, eds., "Resource Management on the Flightdeck," Proceedings of a NASA/Industry Workshop (NASA CP-2120), 1980; and Robert L. Melmreich, Ashleigh C. Merritt, John A. Wilhelm, "The Evolution of Crew Resource Management in Training in Commercial Aviation," *International Journal of Aviation Psychology* 9 (1999): 19–32.

3. Stephen D. Pratt, Susan Mann, Mary Salisbury, et al., "Impact of CRM-Based Team Training on Obstetric Outcomes and Clinicians' Patient Safety Attitudes," *Joint Commission Journal on Quality and Patient Safety* 33, no. 12 (2007): 720–25.

4. See Paul F. Levy, *Goal Play: Leadership Lessons from the Soccer Field* (CreateSpace Independent Publishing Platform, 2012).

5. Zirui Song and Tom Lee, "The Era of Delivery System Reform Begins," *Journal of the American Medical Association* 309, no. 1 (2013): 35–36.

6. *Lean Practices Aid Manufacturers in Recovery,* Compdata Surveys (Dolan Technologies, 2011).

7. Robert Spector and Patrick D. McCarthy, *The Nordstrom Way to Customer Service Excellence: The Handbook for Becoming the "Nordstrom" of Your Industry* (Hoboken, NJ: Wiley, 2012), 253; Paula Godar, "A Wise Choice: Caesars' Bet on Employees Pays Off," Hospitality Net, Jan. 14, 2011, www.hospitalitynet.org/news/154000392/4049796.html; and Tony Hsieh, *Delivering Happiness: A Path to Profits, Passion, and Purpose* (Mundelein: Round Table, 2012).

8. Nicholas Bloom et al., "Management Practices across Firms and Countries," *Academy of Management* 26, no. 1 (2012): 12–33.

9. Through a variety of techniques, they conclude that the process changes lead to improved outcomes, rather than the other way around.

10. The impact of a one-point increase in management quality is presented in *Management in Healthcare: What Good Practice Really Means* (London: McKinsey and Company, 2010), available at: http://worldmanagementsurvey.org/wp-content/images/2010/10/Management_in_Healthcare_Report_2010.pdf. The numbers in the text are scaled to an improvement of 0.3.

11. *Avastin: Scientific Discussion* (European Medicines Agency, 2005), www.ema.europa.eu/docs/en_GB/document_library/EPAR_-_Scientific_Discussion/human/000582/WC500029262.pdf.

12. Peter B. Bach, Leonard B. Saltz, and Robert E. Wittes, "In Cancer Care, Cost Matters," *New York Times,* Oct. 14, 2012. In response to this decision, Sanofi cut the price of Zaltrap. See Andrew Pollack, "Sanofi Halves Price of Cancer Drug Zaltrap after Sloan-Kettering Rejection," *New York Times,* Nov. 8, 2012.

13. Helen Pidd, "Avastin Prolongs Life but Drug Is Too Expensive for NHS Patients, Says Nice," *Guardian,* Aug. 23, 2010.

14. "NICE Recommends Abiraterone and Erlotinib," NHS: National Institute for Health and Clinical Excellence, June 26, 2012; "Abiraterone for Castration-Resistant Metastatic Prostate Cancer Previously Treated with a Docetaxel-Containing Regimen," National Institute for Health and Clinical Excellence, June 2012; and Sarah Boseley, "Cancer Drug 'Too Expensive for NHS,'" *Guardian,* Feb. 1, 2012.

15. Andrew Pollack, "Medicare Will Continue to Cover 2 Expensive Cancer Drugs," *New York Times,* June 30, 2011.

16. IMS Institute for Healthcare Informatics, *The Use of Medicines in the United States: Review of 2010* (IMS Health, 2011).

17. "Medicare Q&A: Saving Medicare," House of Representatives Committee on the Budget, http://budget.house.gov/settingtherecordstraight/savingmedicare.htm.

18. Edward P. Lazear, "Performance Pay and Productivity," *American Economic Review* 90, no. 5 (2000): 1346–61.

19. Steven Kaplan and Josh Rauh, "Wall Street and Main Street: What Contributes to the Rise in the Highest Incomes?" *Review of Financial Studies* 23 (2000): 1004–50.

20. "Cystic Fibrosis," National Center for Biotechnology Information, U.S. National Library of Medicine, May 16, 2012; "Research Milestones," Cystic Fibrosis Foundation, Nov. 20, 2012, www.cff.org/research/ResearchMilestones/; "About Cystic Fibrosis: What You Need to Know," Cystic Fibrosis Foundation, www.cff.org/AboutCF/. A drug, Kalydeco, was recently approved to treat some patients with CF. Because it was genetically targeted, the drug seems to work well—with good efficacy and few side effects. The drug costs $294,000 for a year of treatment.

21. Atul Gawande, "The Bell Curve," in *Better: A Surgeon's Notes on Performance* (New York: Metropolitan, 2007), 227.

22. Anita Tucker and Amy Edmondson, *Cincinnati Children's Hospital Medical Center,* case study (Harvard Business School, 2010).

23. David Blumenthal, "Why Be a Meaningful User?" Health IT Buzz, Apr. 27, 2010, www.healthit.gov/buzz-blog/meaningful-use/why-meaningful-user/.

24. Catherine M. DesRoches et al., "Electronic Health Records in Ambulatory Care—A National Survey of Physicians," *New England Journal of Medicine* 359 (2008): 50–60.

25. Eric Jamoom et al., *Physician Adoption of Electronic Health Record Systems: United States, 2011,* NCHS data brief no. 98 (Hyattsville, MD: National Center for Health Statistics, 2012).

26. Claudia Goldin and Lawrence F. Katz, *The Race between Education and Technology* (Cambridge, MA: Harvard University Press, 2008).

27. C. Kenney and Donald M. Berwick, *Transforming Health Care: Virginia Mason Medical Center's Pursuit of the Perfect Patient Experience* (New York: CRC, 2011).

28. Anupam B. Jena et al., "Malpractice Risk according to Physician Specialty," *New England Journal of Medicine* 365, no. 7 (2011): 629–36.

29. "Tort Reform," U.S. Congressional Budget Office, Oct. 9, 2009, www.cbo.gov/sites/default/files/cbofiles/ftpdocs/106xx/doc10641/10-09-tort_reform.pdf.

30. For a review, see Katherine Baicker, Elliott S. Fisher, and Amitabh Chandra, "Malpractice Liability Costs and the Practice of Medicine in the Medicare Program," *Health Affairs* 26, no. 3 (2007): 841–52.

31. Teresa M. Waters et al., "Impact of State Tort Reforms on Physician Malpractice Payments," *Health Affairs* 26, no. 2 (2007): 500–509; Douglas W. Elmendorf, Letter to Honorable Orrin G. Hatch, Oct. 9, 2009, Congressional Budget Office, www.cbo.gov/sites/default/files/cbofiles/ftpdocs/106xx/doc10641/10-09-tort_reform.pdf. The savings are estimated to be $41 billion, off a base of $2.4 trillion of medical spending over the next decade.

32. Allen Kachalia et al., "Liability Claims and Costs Before and After Implementation of a Medical Error Disclosure Program," *Annals of Internal Medicine* 153, no. 4 (2010): 213–21.

33. Blue Cross Blue Shield Foundation, *Summary of Chapter 224 of the Acts of 2012* (Boston, MA: Blue Cross Blue Shield Foundation, 2012).

34. "Remarks by the President at the Annual Conference of the American Medical Association," White House, June 15, 2009, www.whitehouse.gov/the-press-office/remarks-president-annual-conference-american-medical-association.

35. Michelle Mello and Allen Kachalia, *Evaluation of Options for Medical Malpractice System Reform* (Washington, DC: Medicare Payment Advisory Commission, 2010).

36. Gordon H. Smith, "Maine's Medical Liability Demonstration Project—Linking Practice Guidelines to Liability Protection," *Virtual Mentor—American Medical Association Journal of Ethics* 13, no. 11 (2011): 792–95.

37. Linda L. LeCraw, "Use of Clinical Practice Guidelines in Medical Malpractice Litigation," *Journal of Oncology Practice* 3, no. 5 (2007): 254.

8. HOW LONG WILL IT TAKE?

1. Ernst Berndt et al., "Medical Care Prices and Output," in Anthony Culyer and Joseph P. Newhouse, eds., *Handbook of Health Economics,* vol. 1A (Amsterdam: Elsevier; 2000), 119–80.

2. Technically, the target is the growth of potential gross state product—which is essentially the growth of the economy assuming there are no recessions or recovery from recession.

3. Joseph P. Newhouse, "Medical Care Costs: How Much Welfare Loss?" *Journal of Economic Perspectives* 6, no. 3 (1992): 3–21.

4. Richard M.J. Bohmer, *Designing Care: Aligning the Nature and Management of Health Care* (Boston, MA: Harvard Business Review Press, 2009).

INDEX

Note: Tables and figures are indicated by *t* or *f* after the page number.